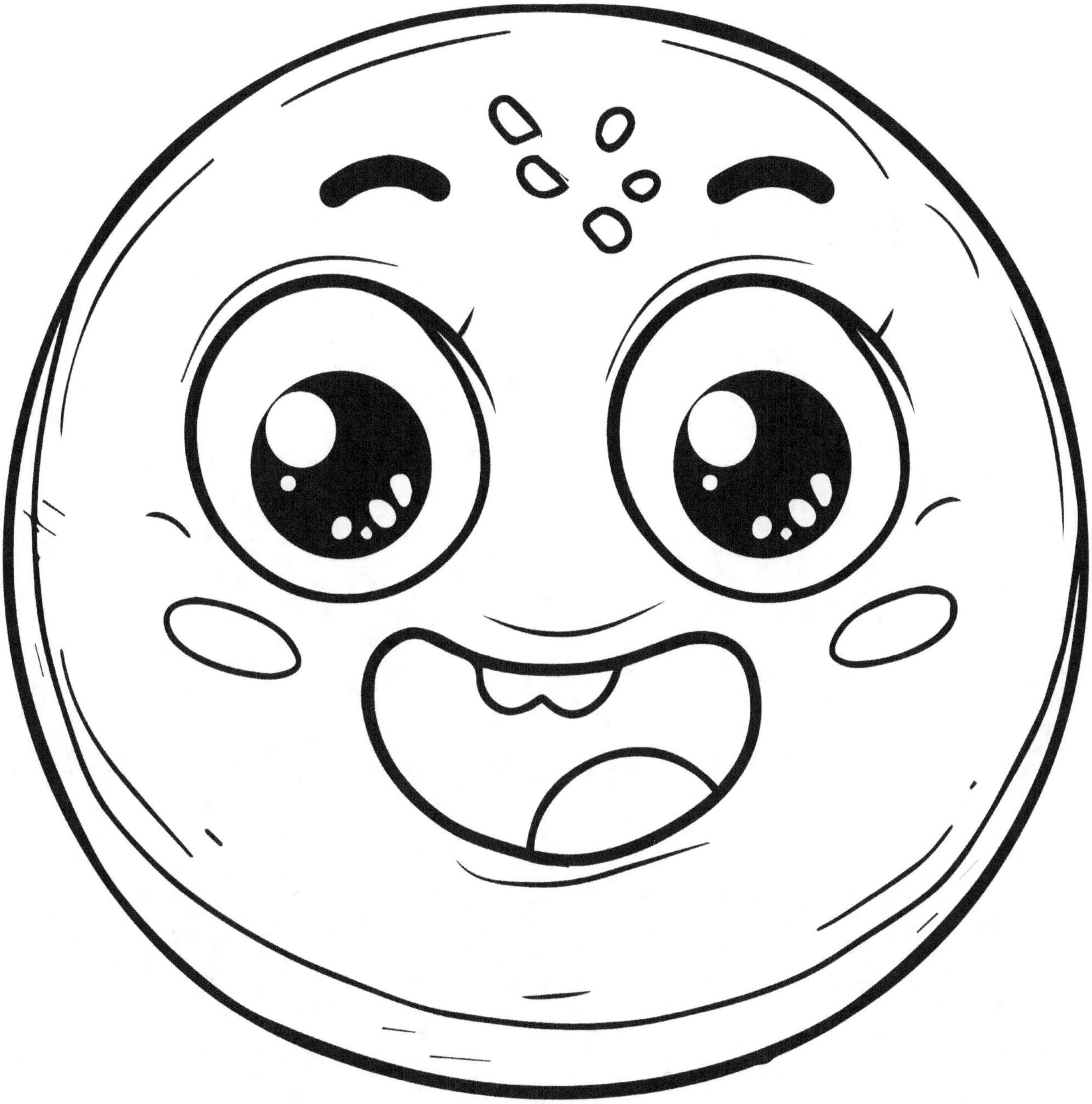

Smile

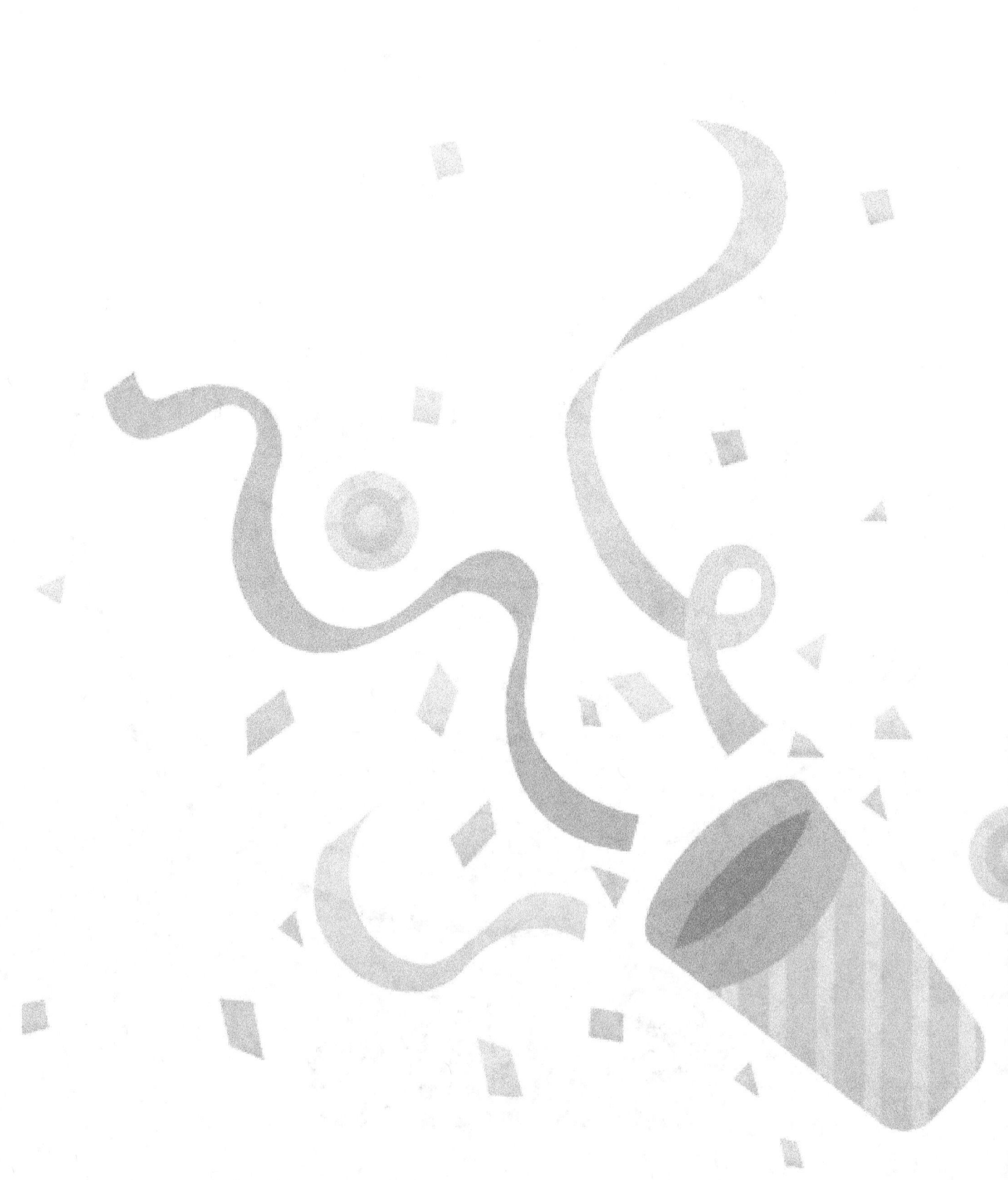

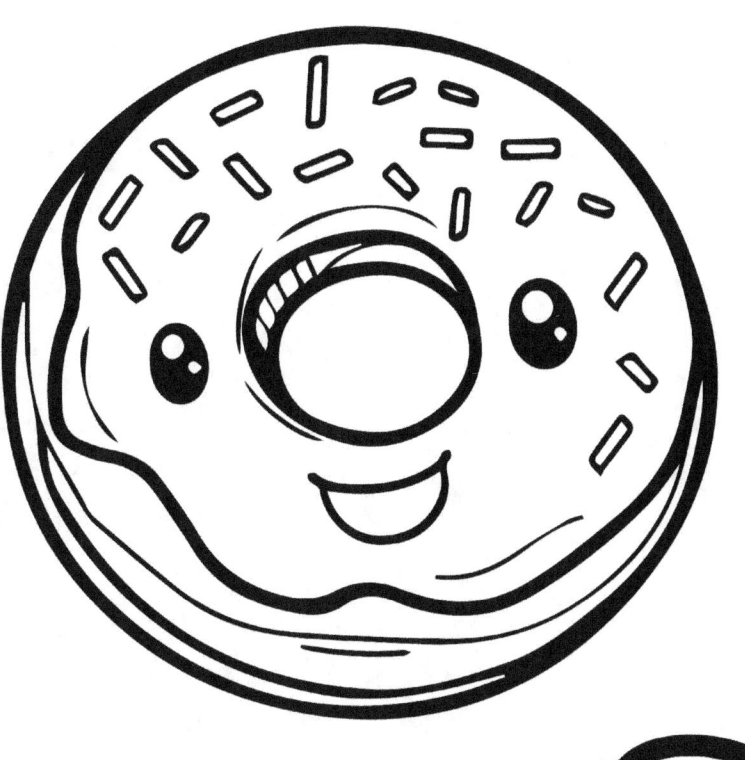

Sibling

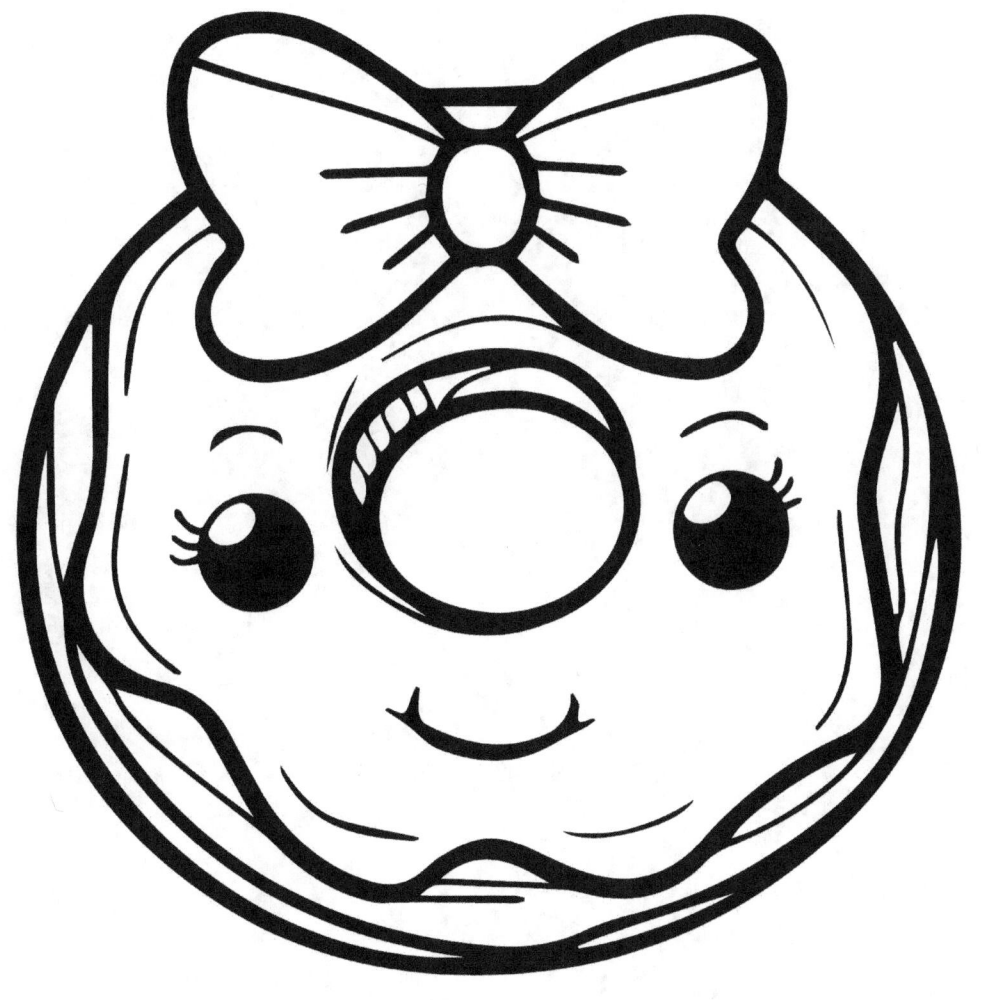

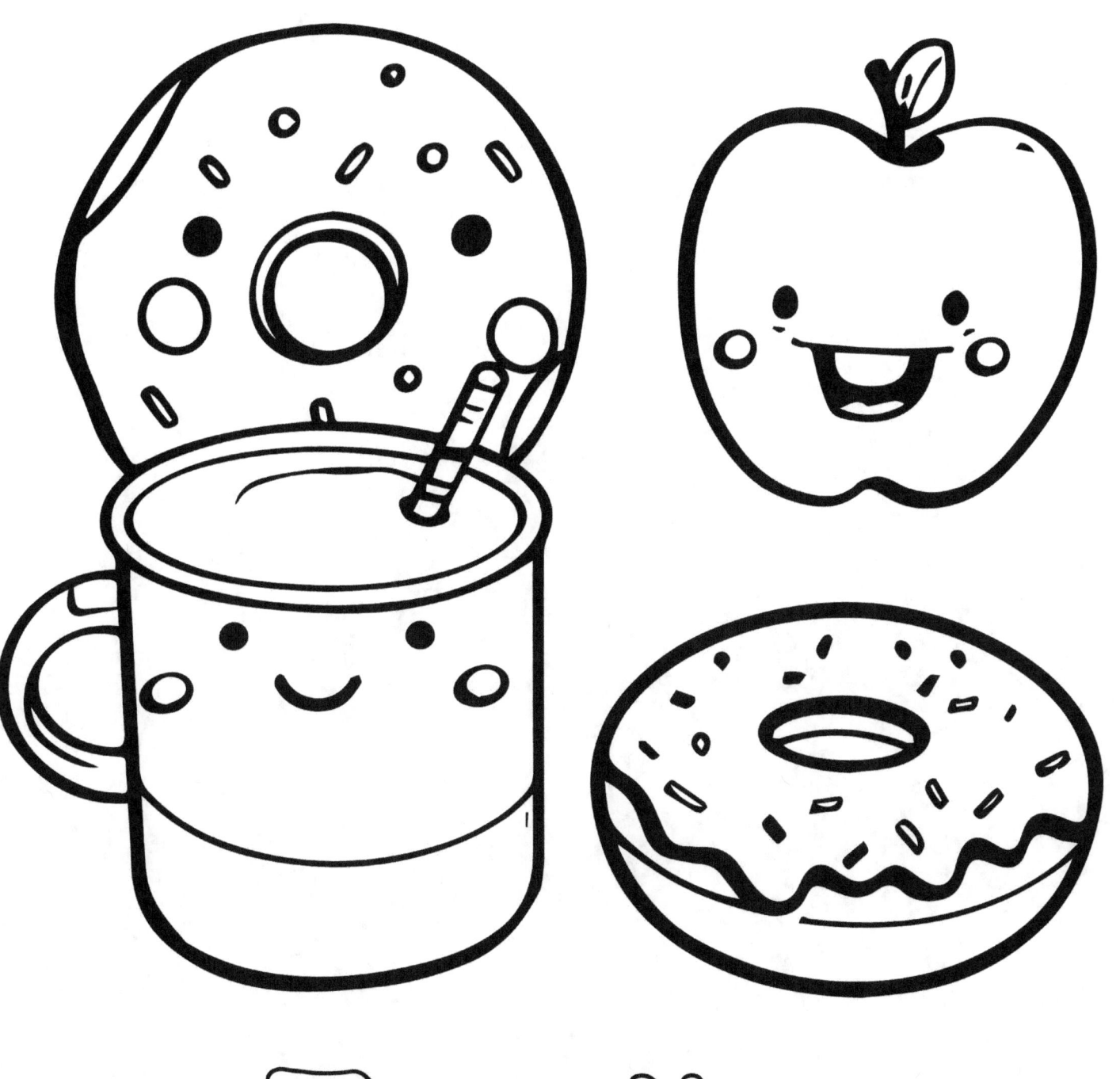

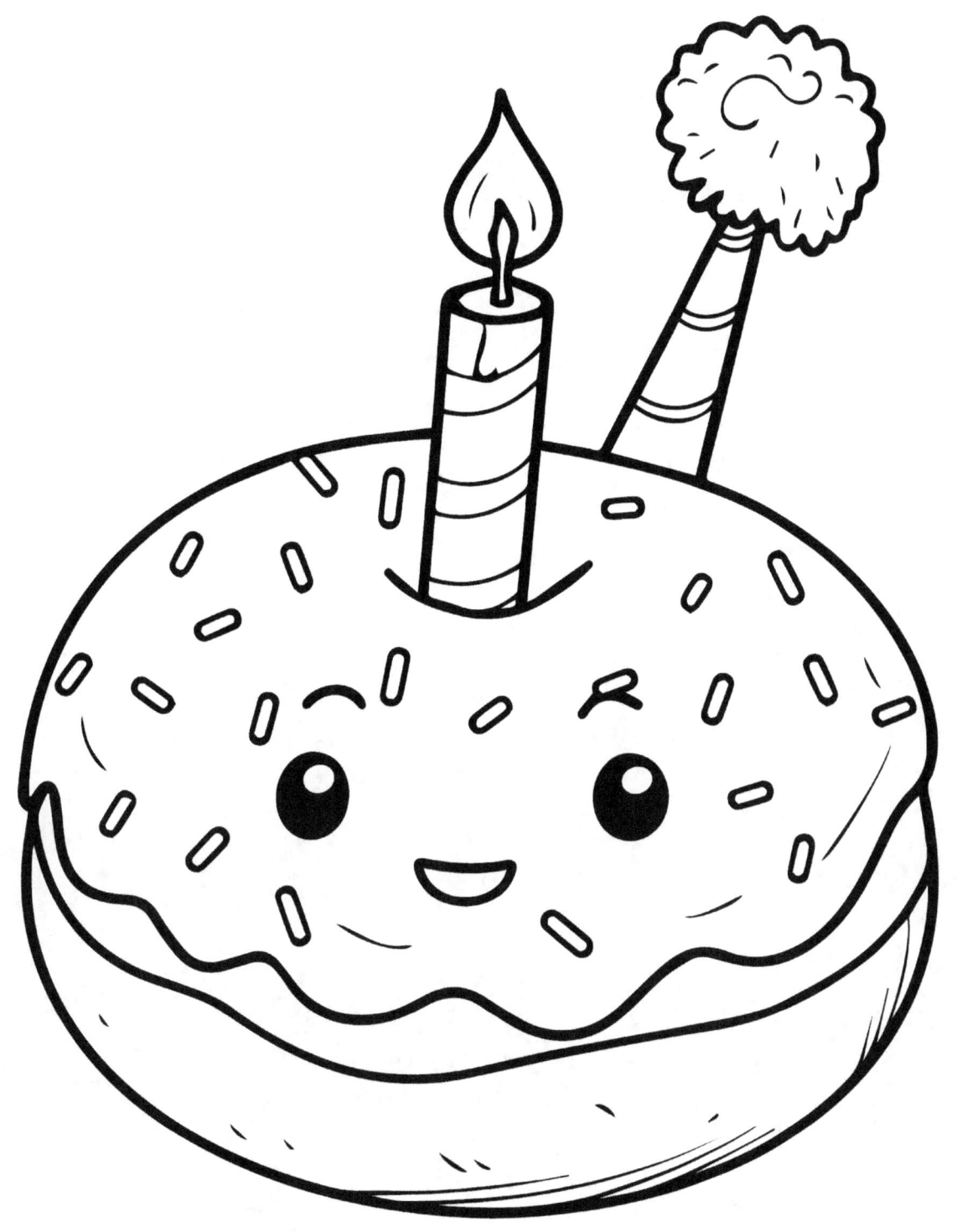

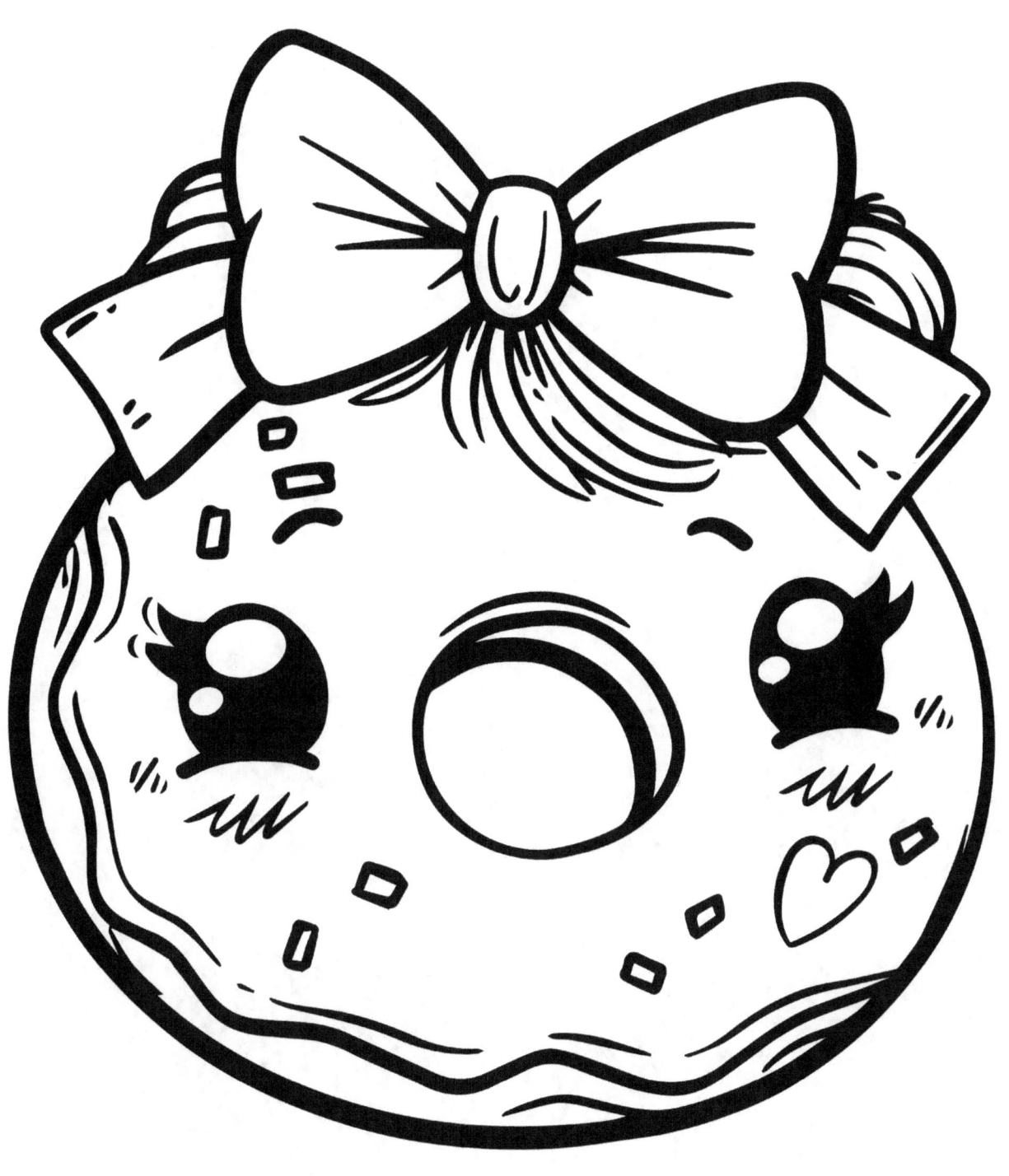

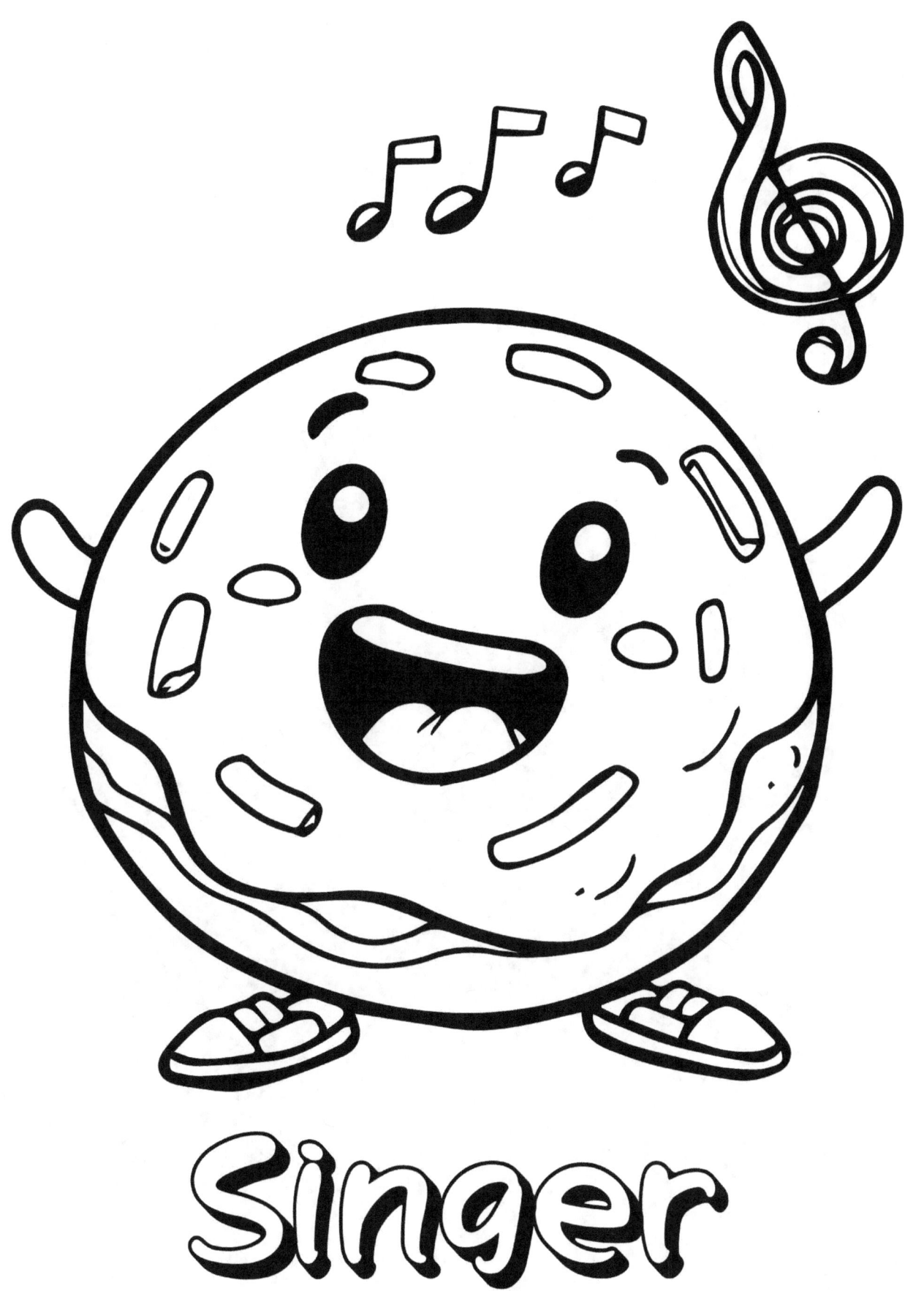

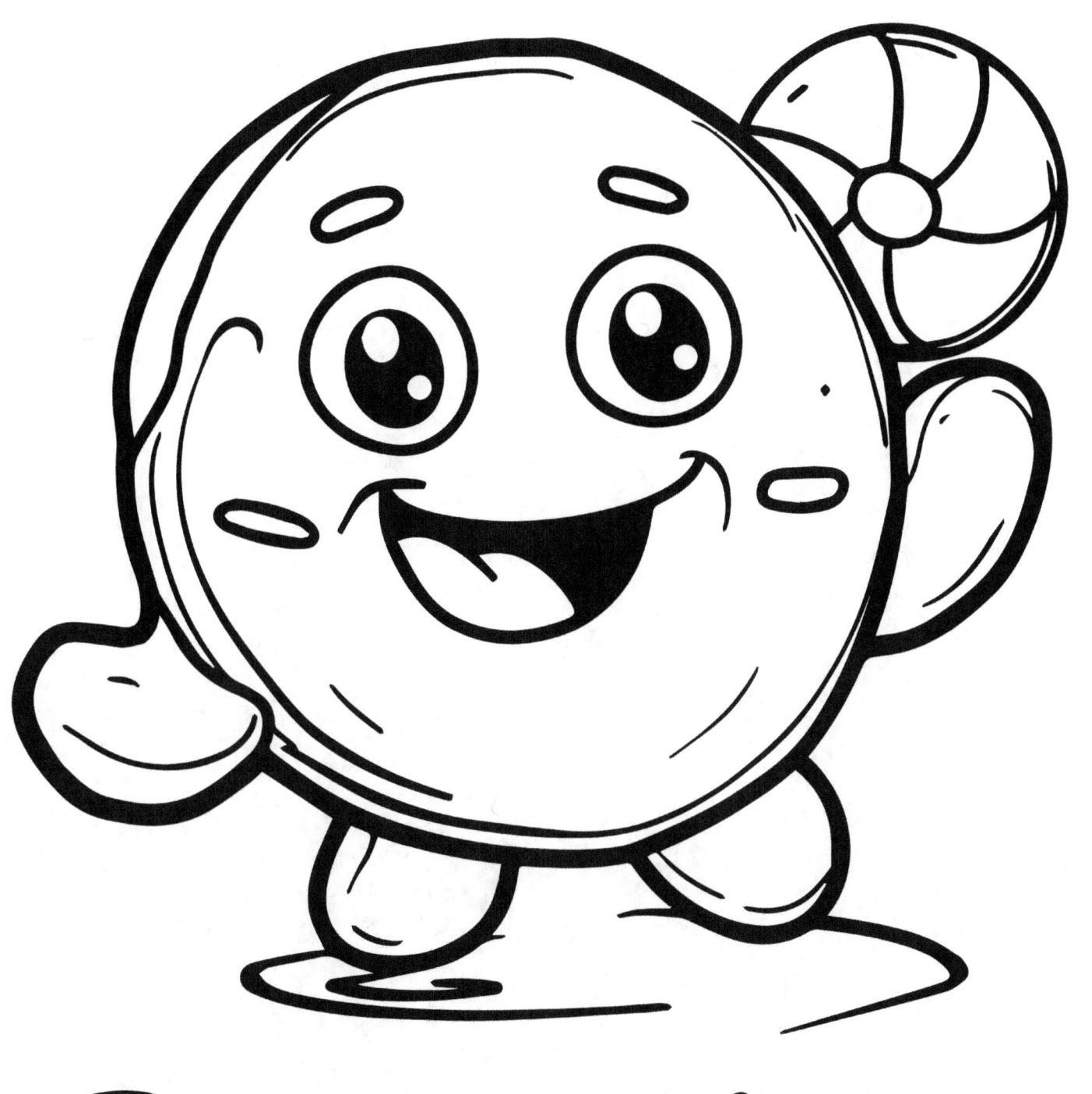

Basketball

Snowman

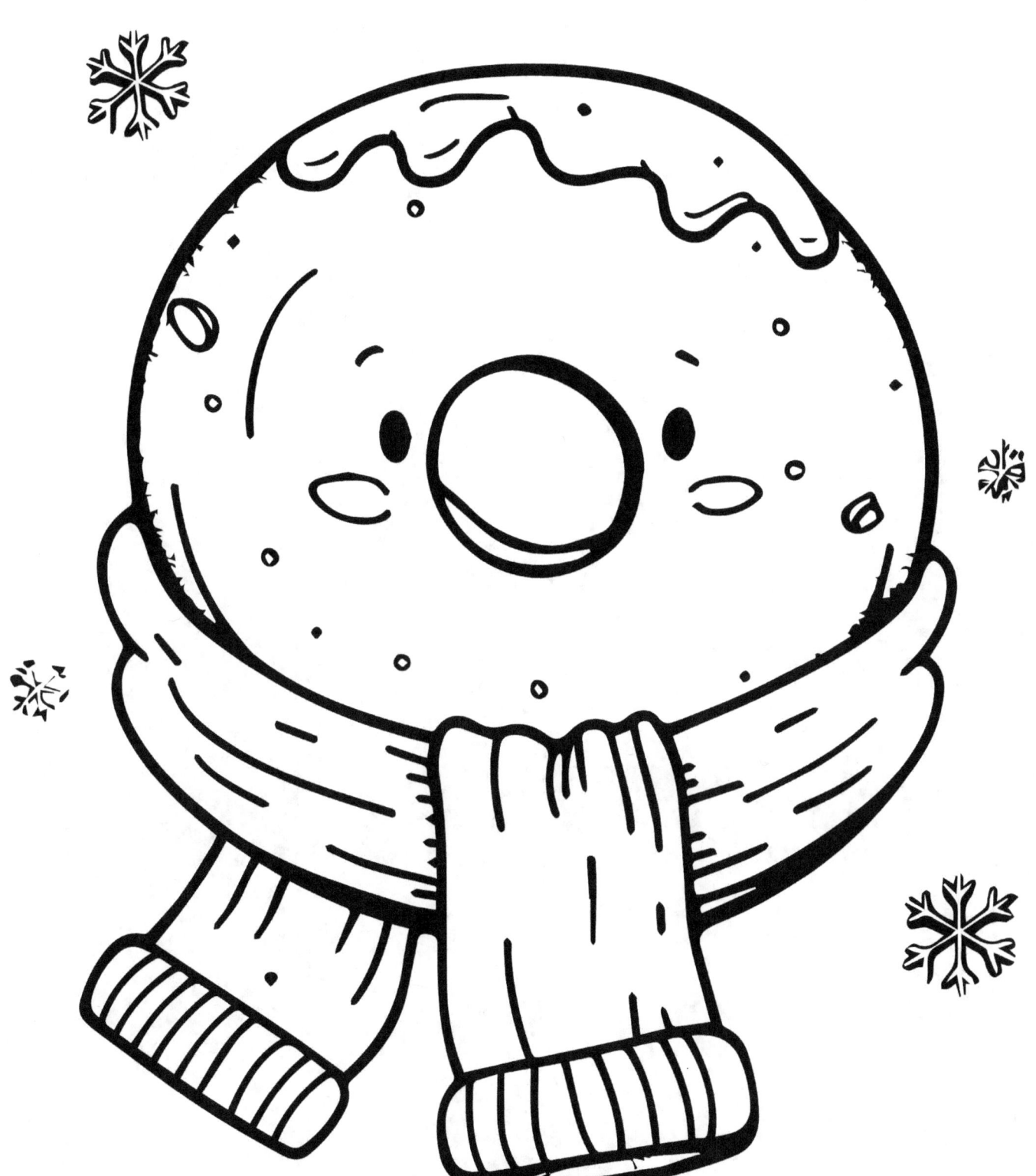

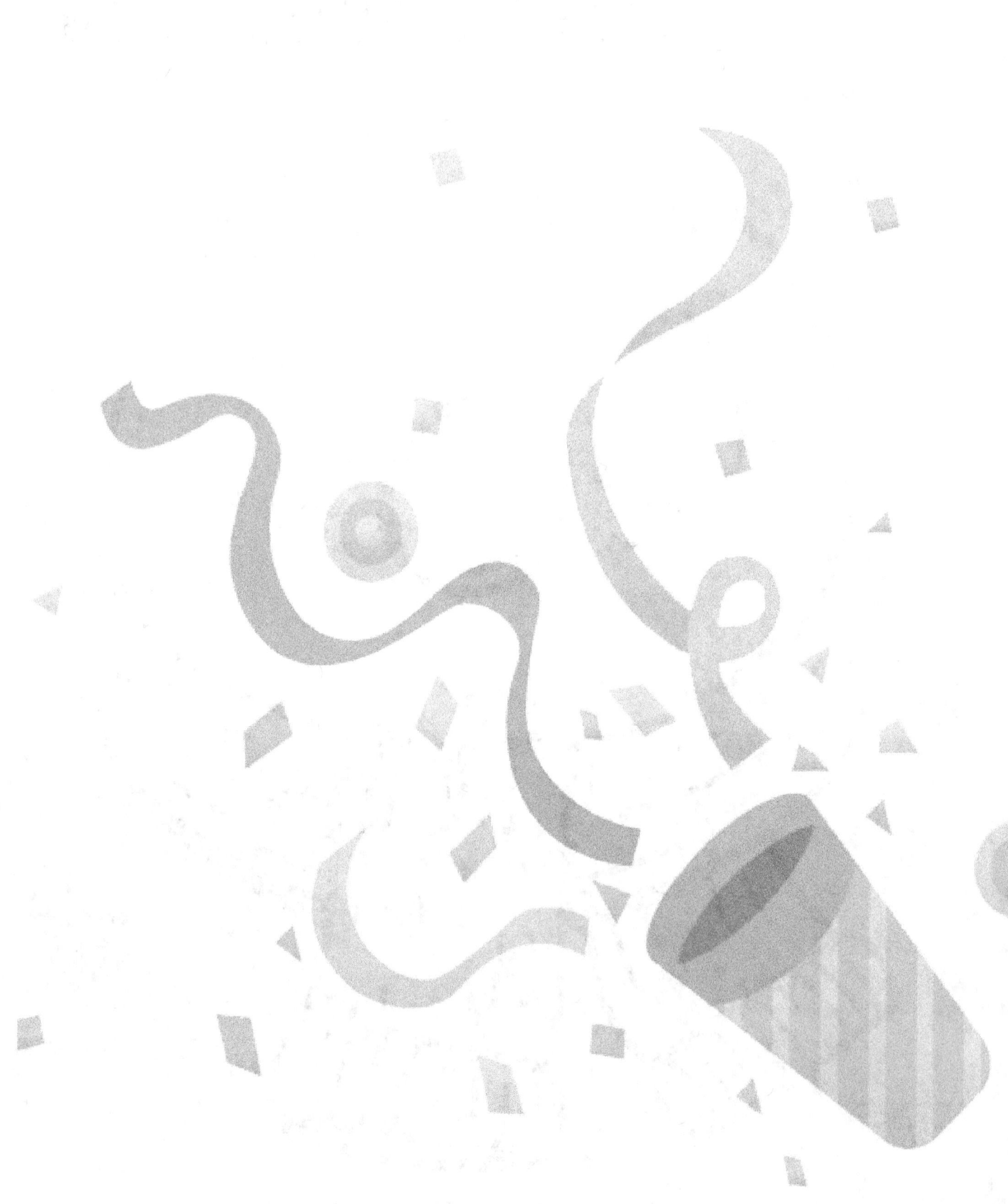

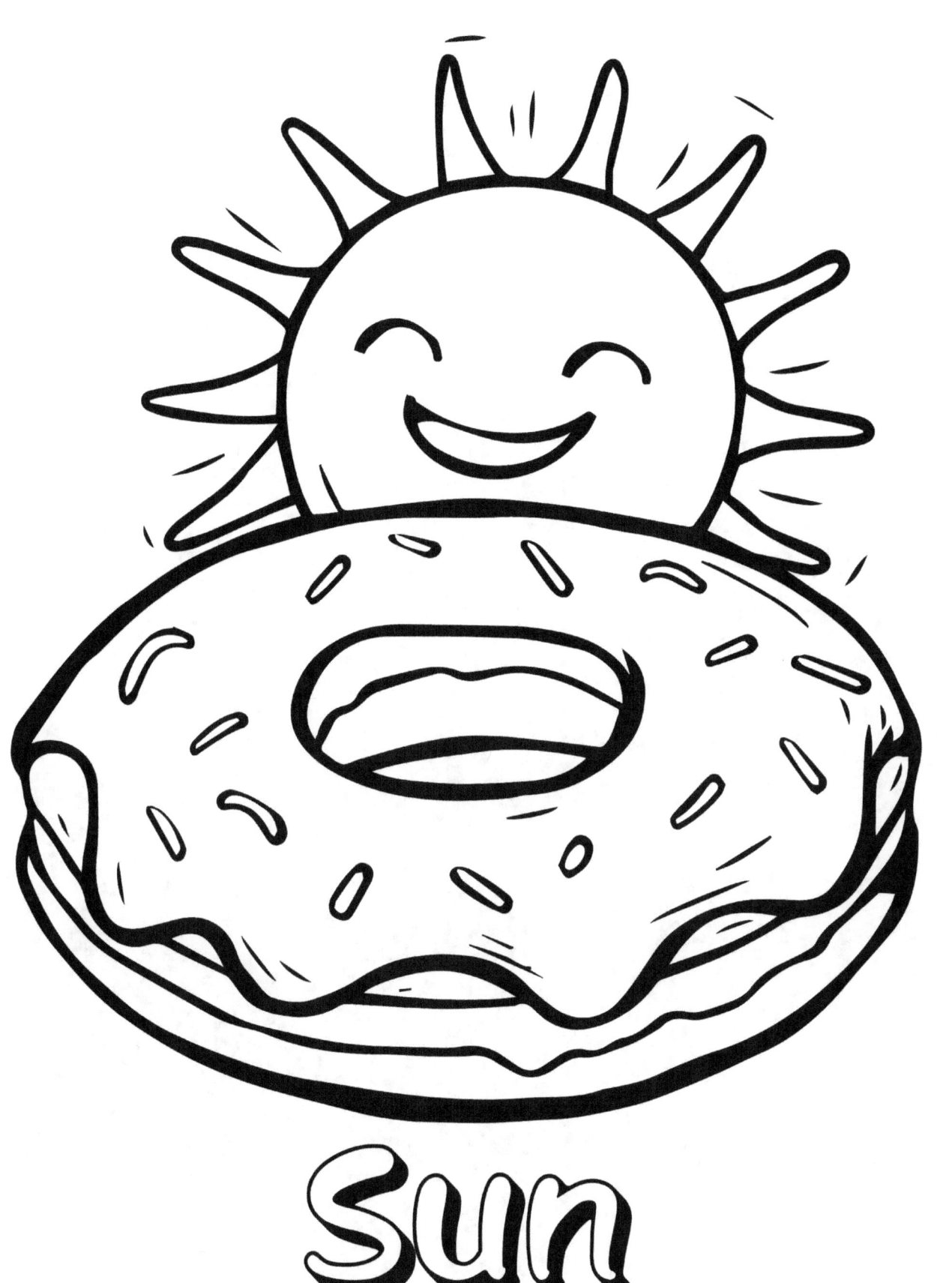

Guitar

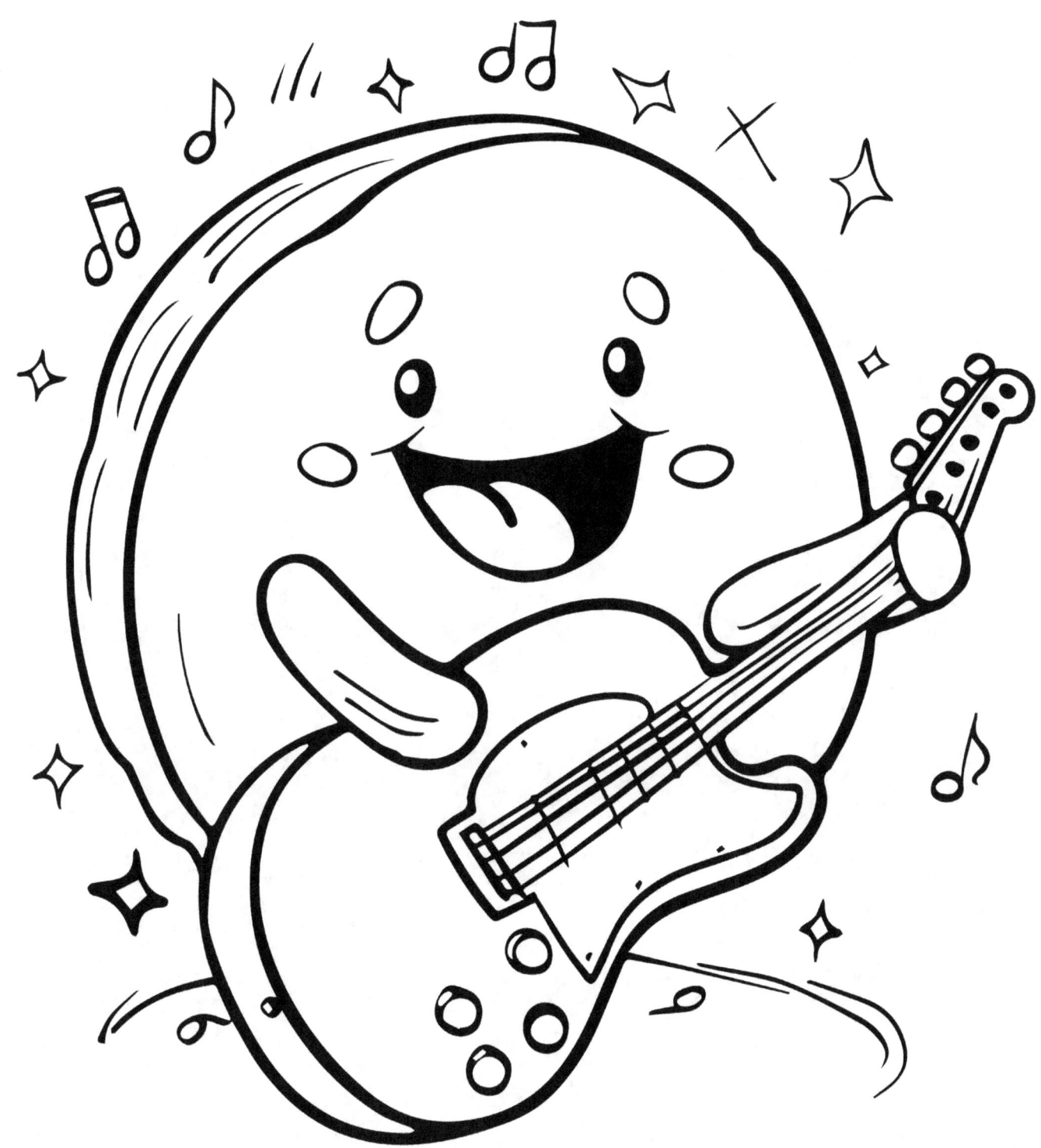

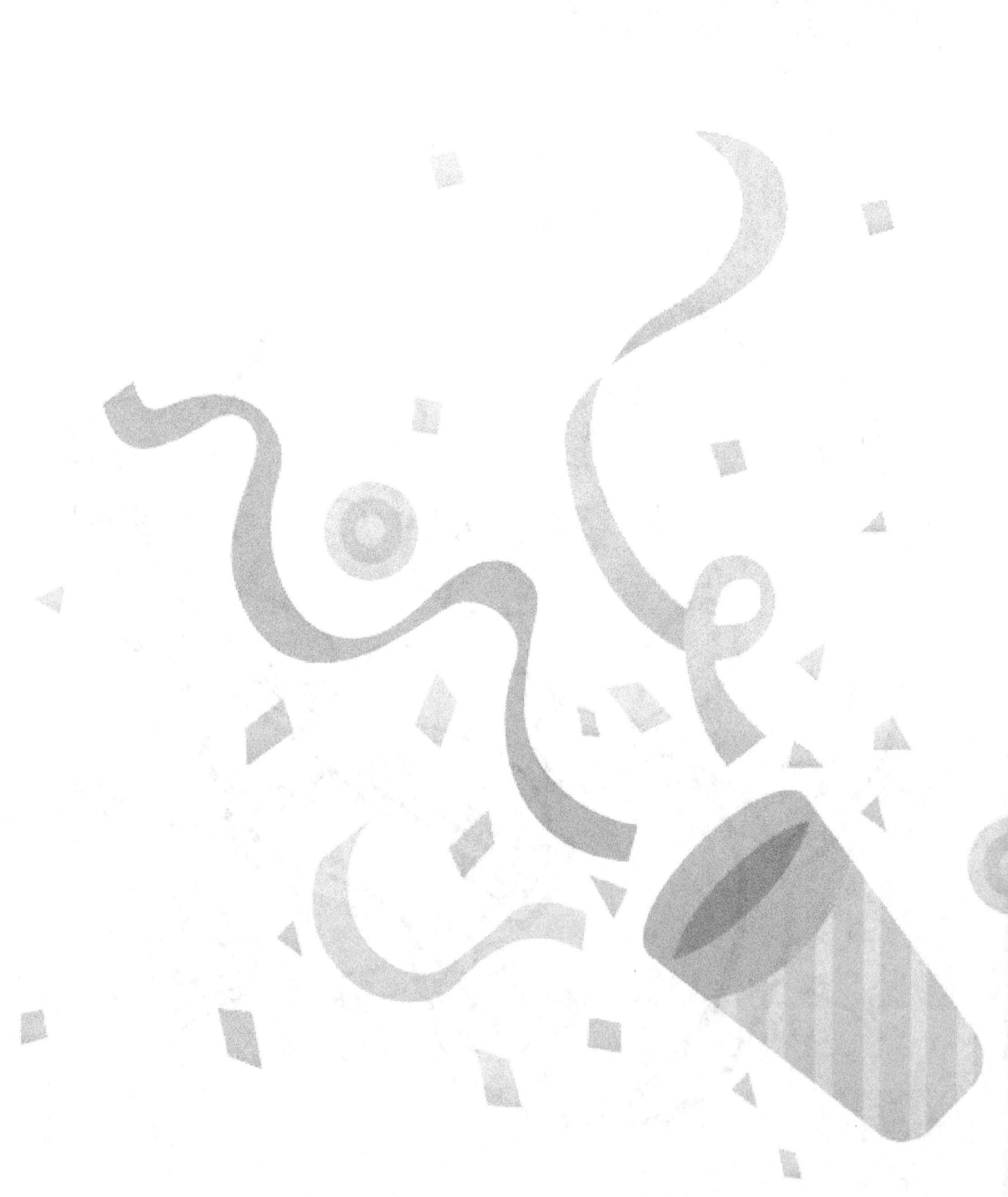

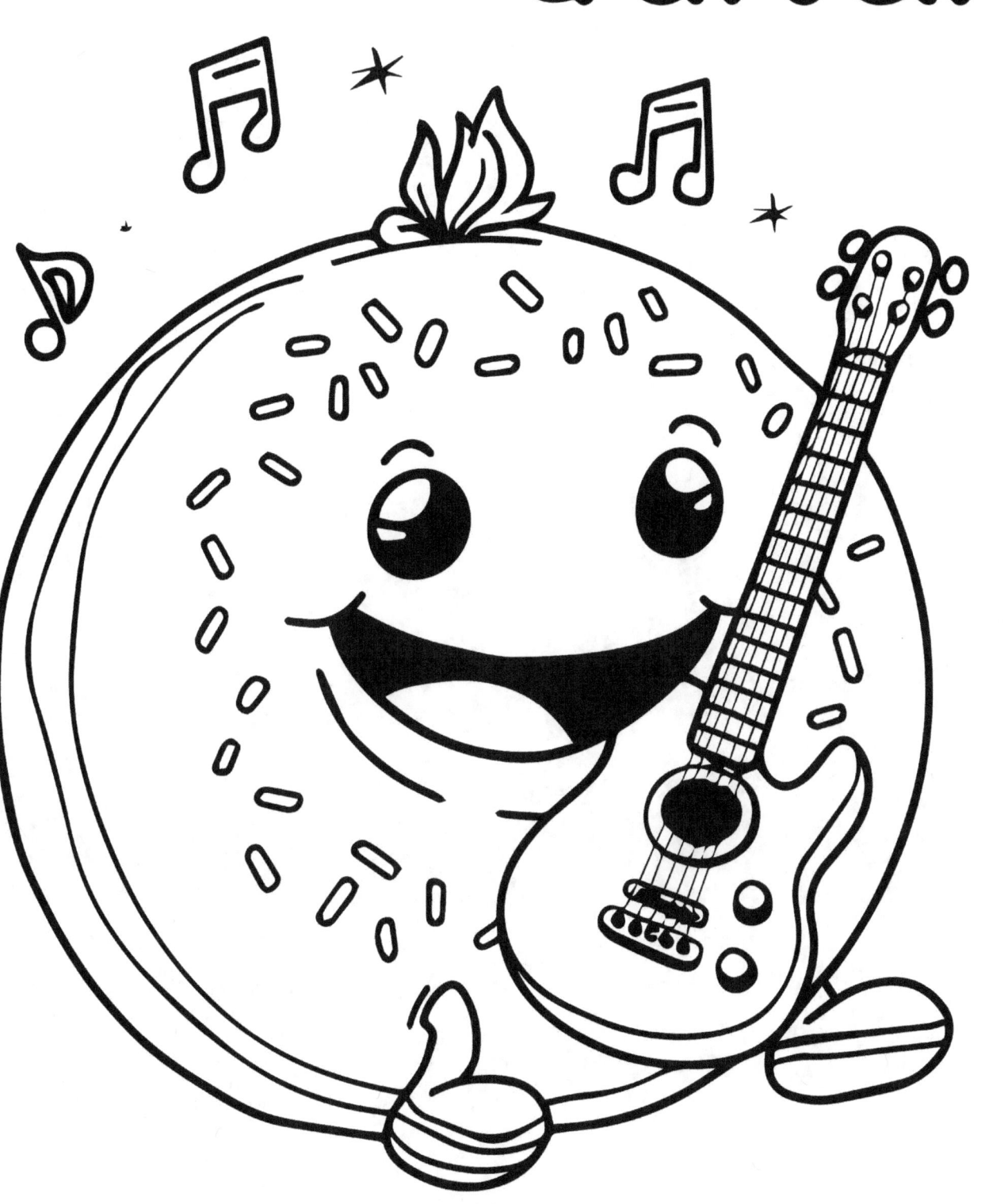

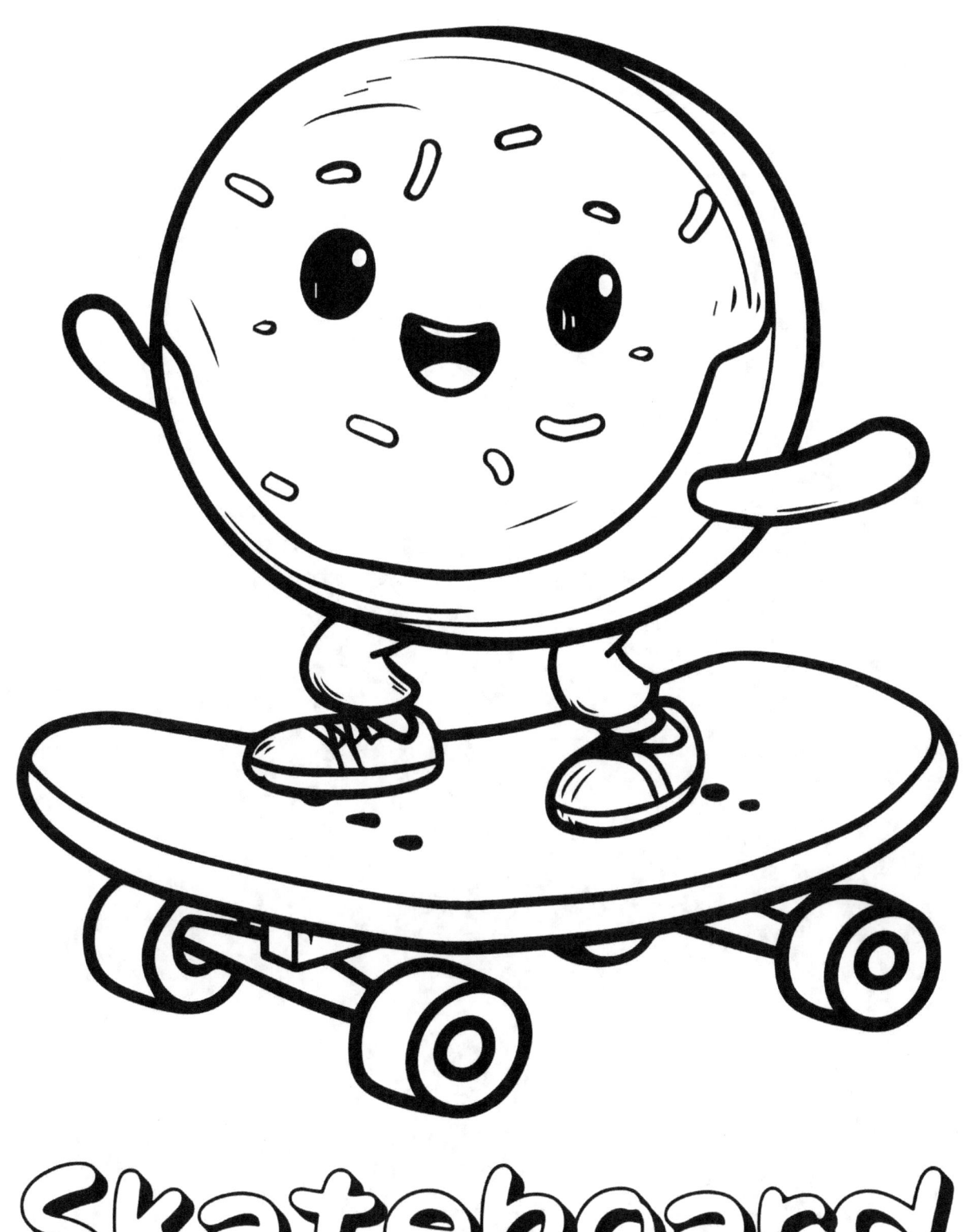

Skateboard

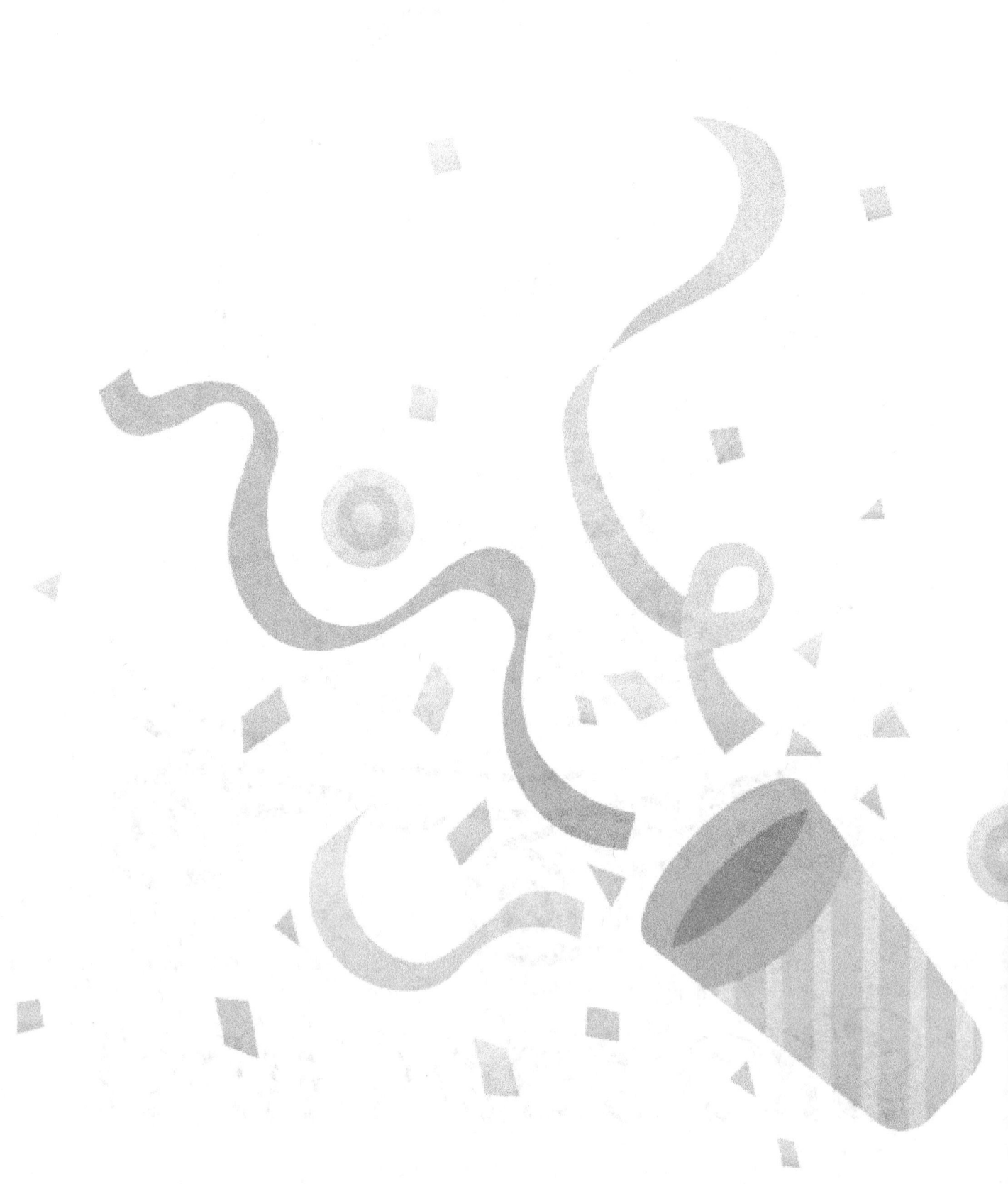

Rainbow

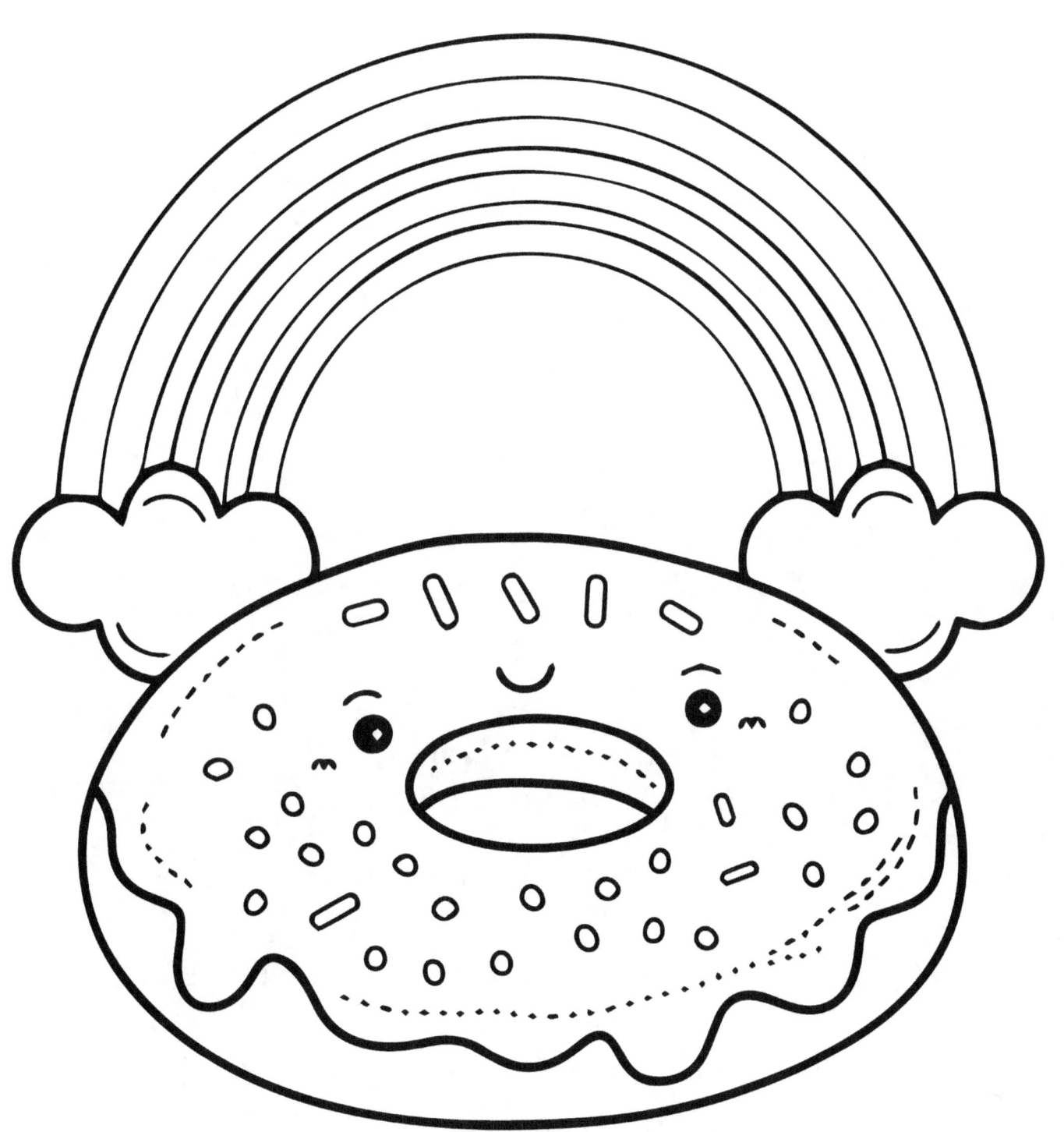

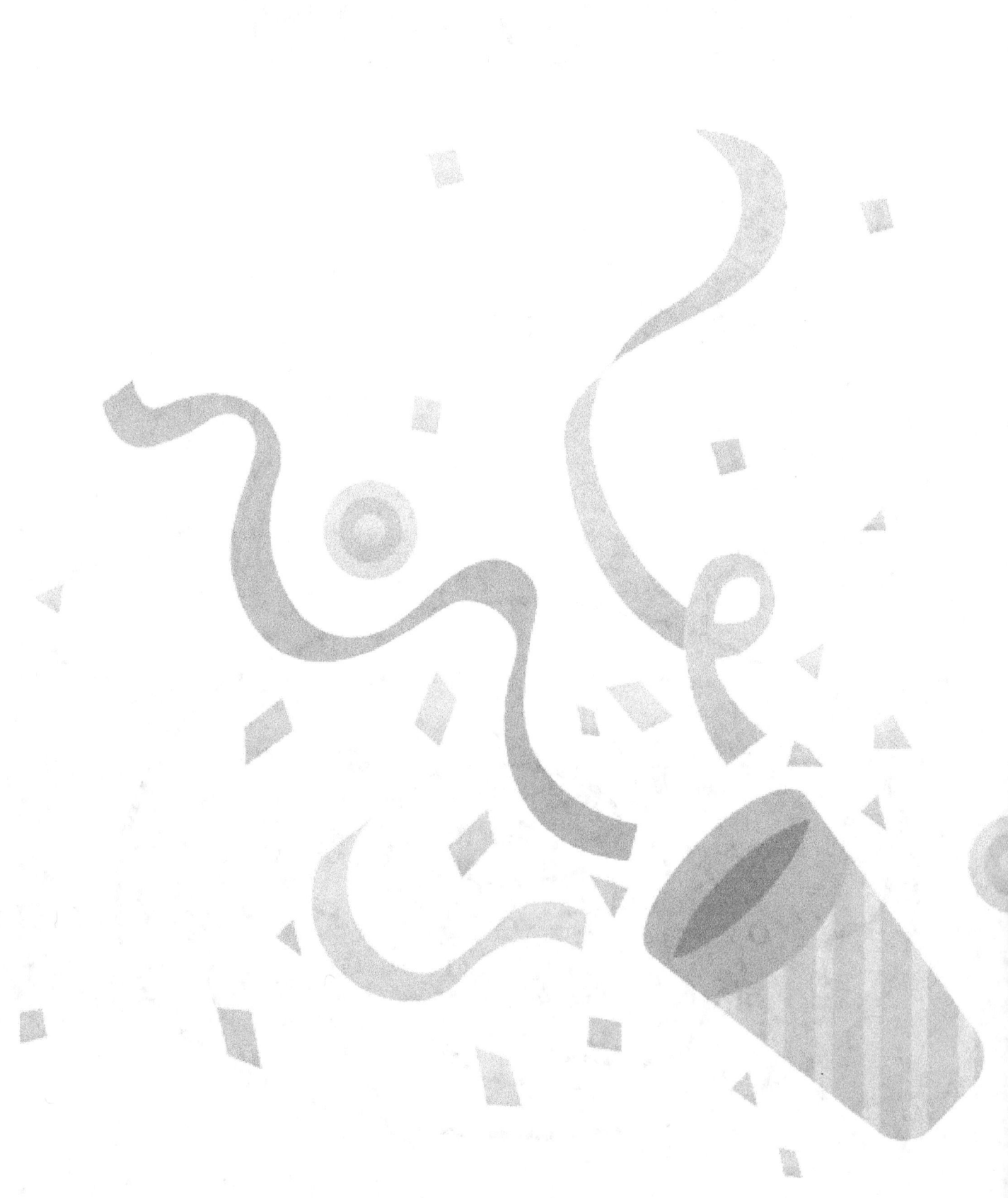

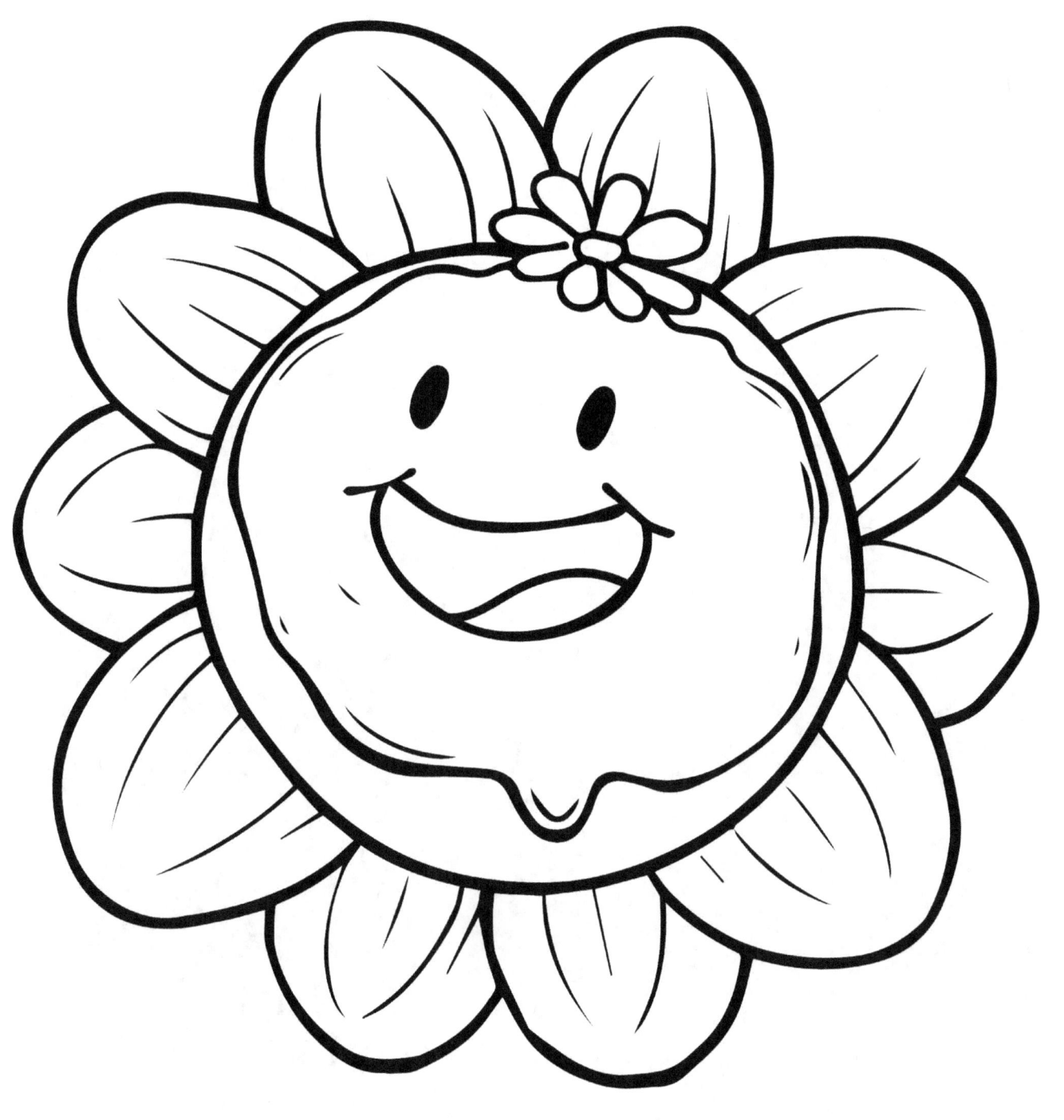

Flower

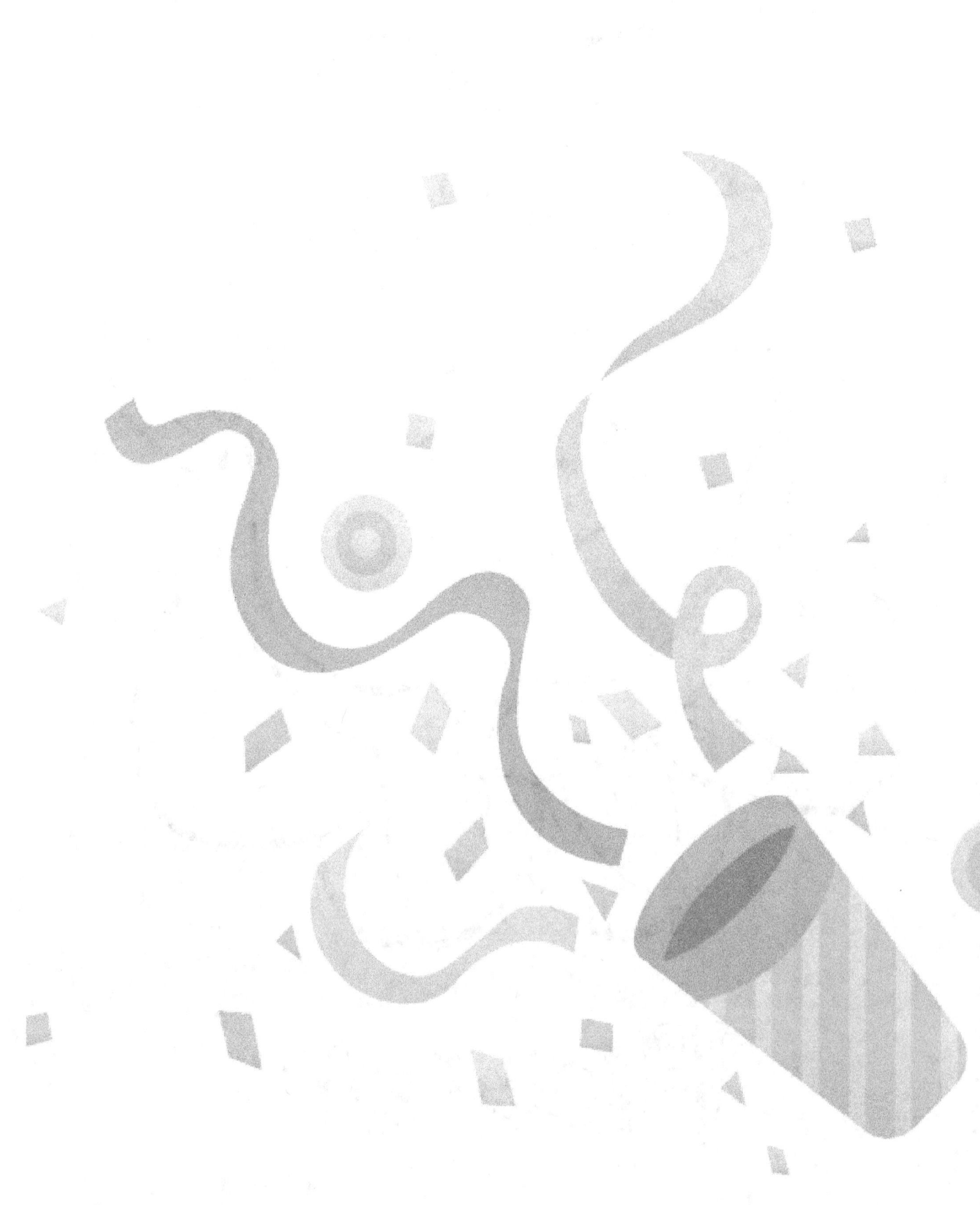

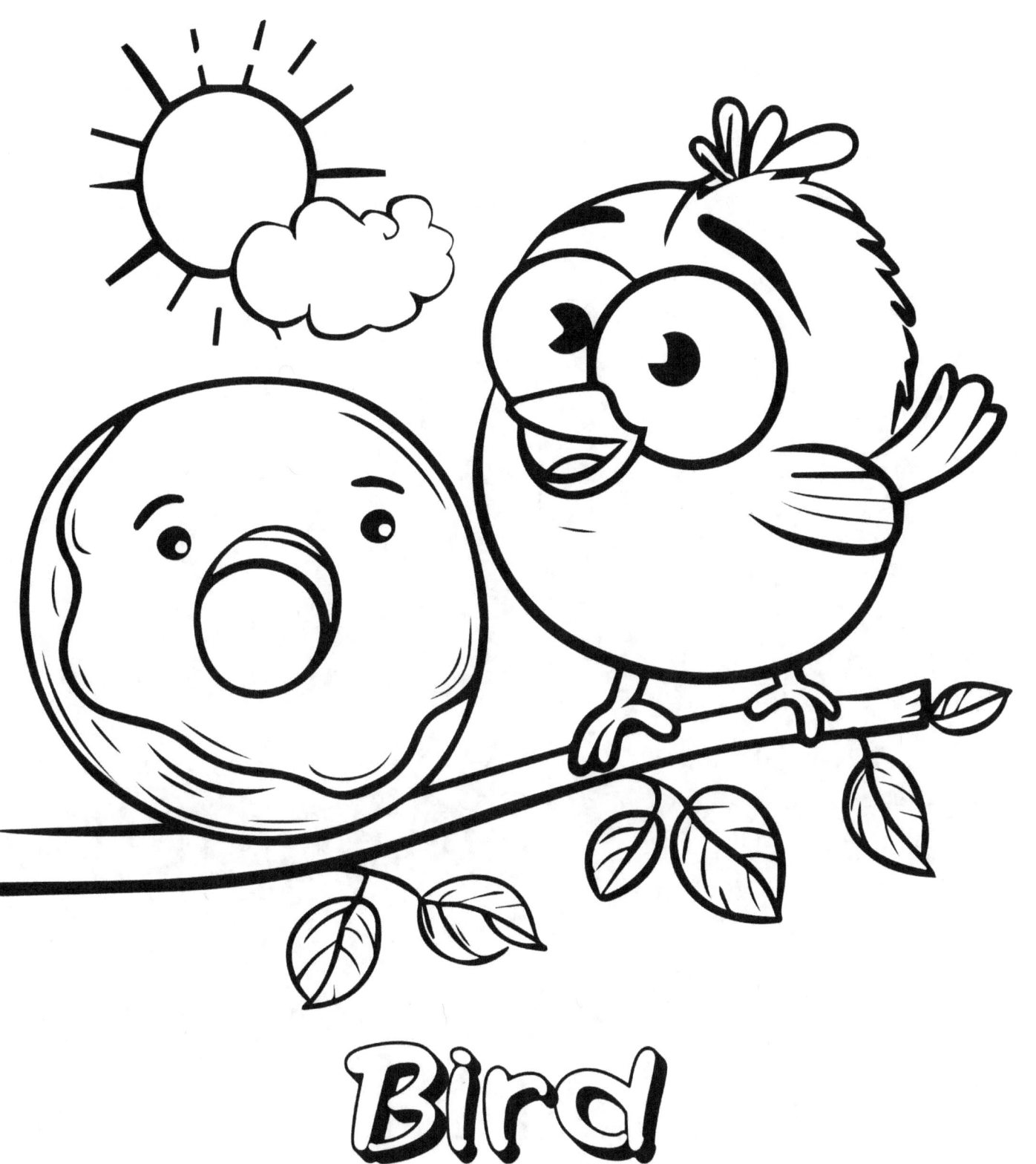

Bird

Painter

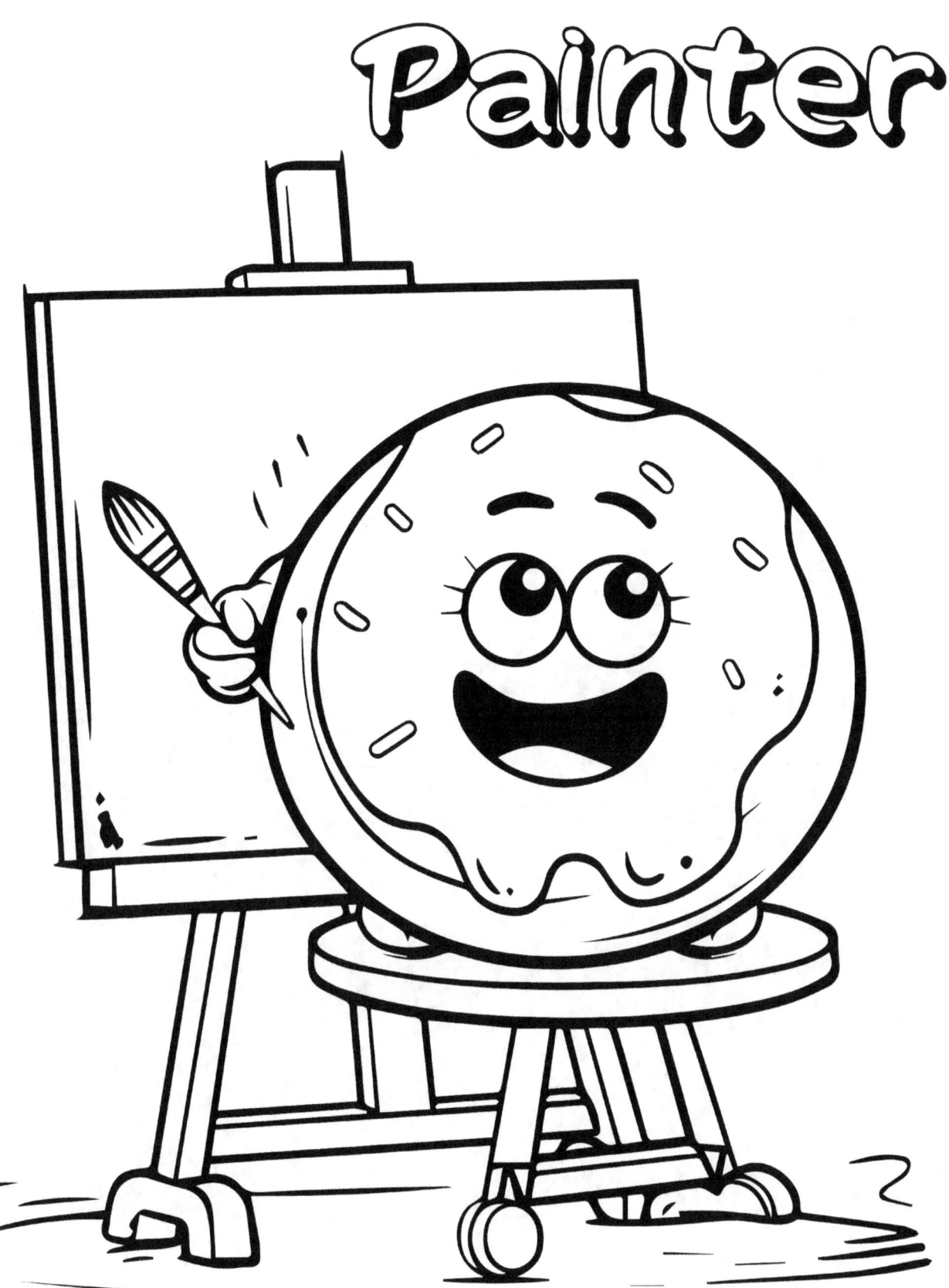

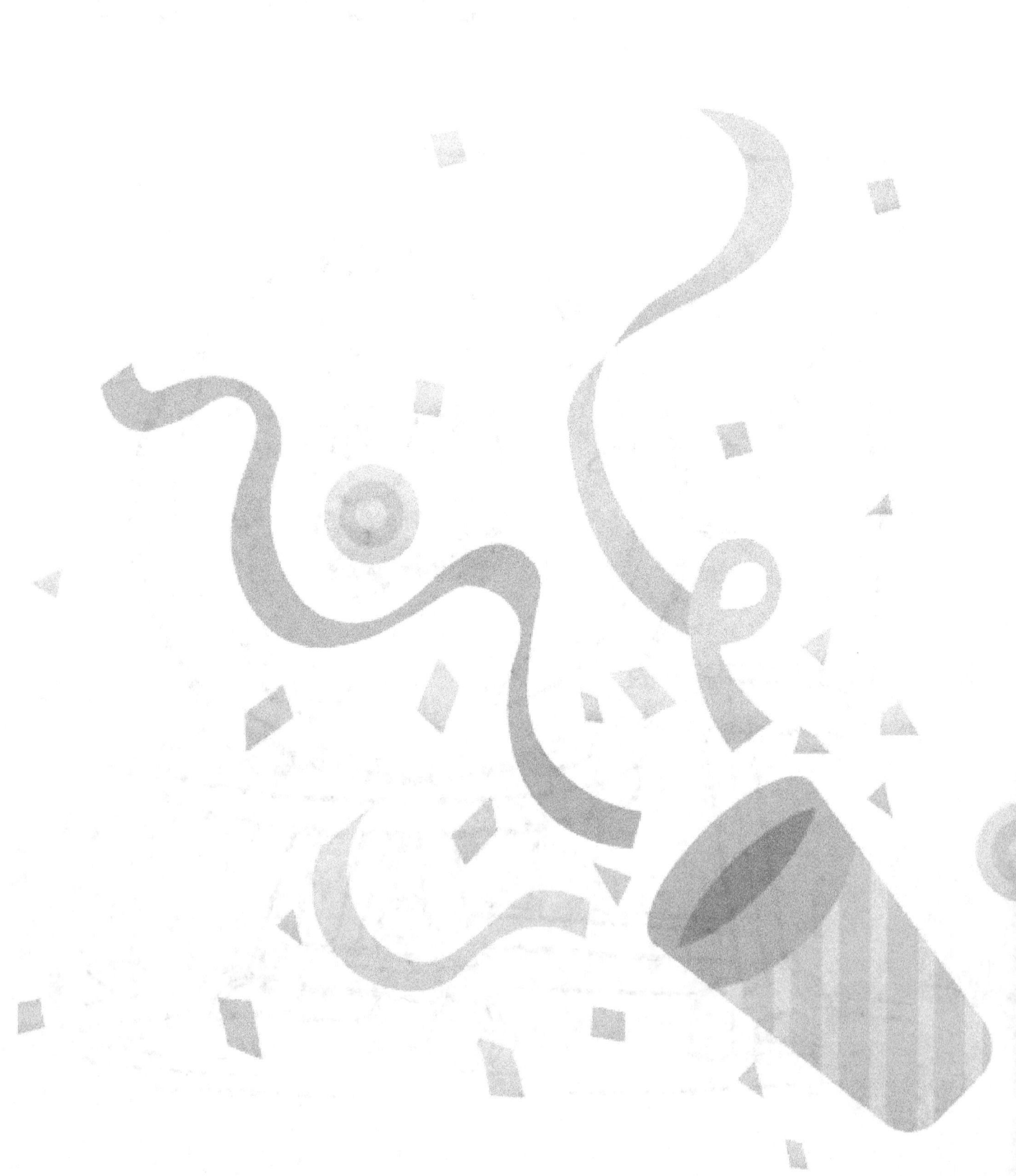

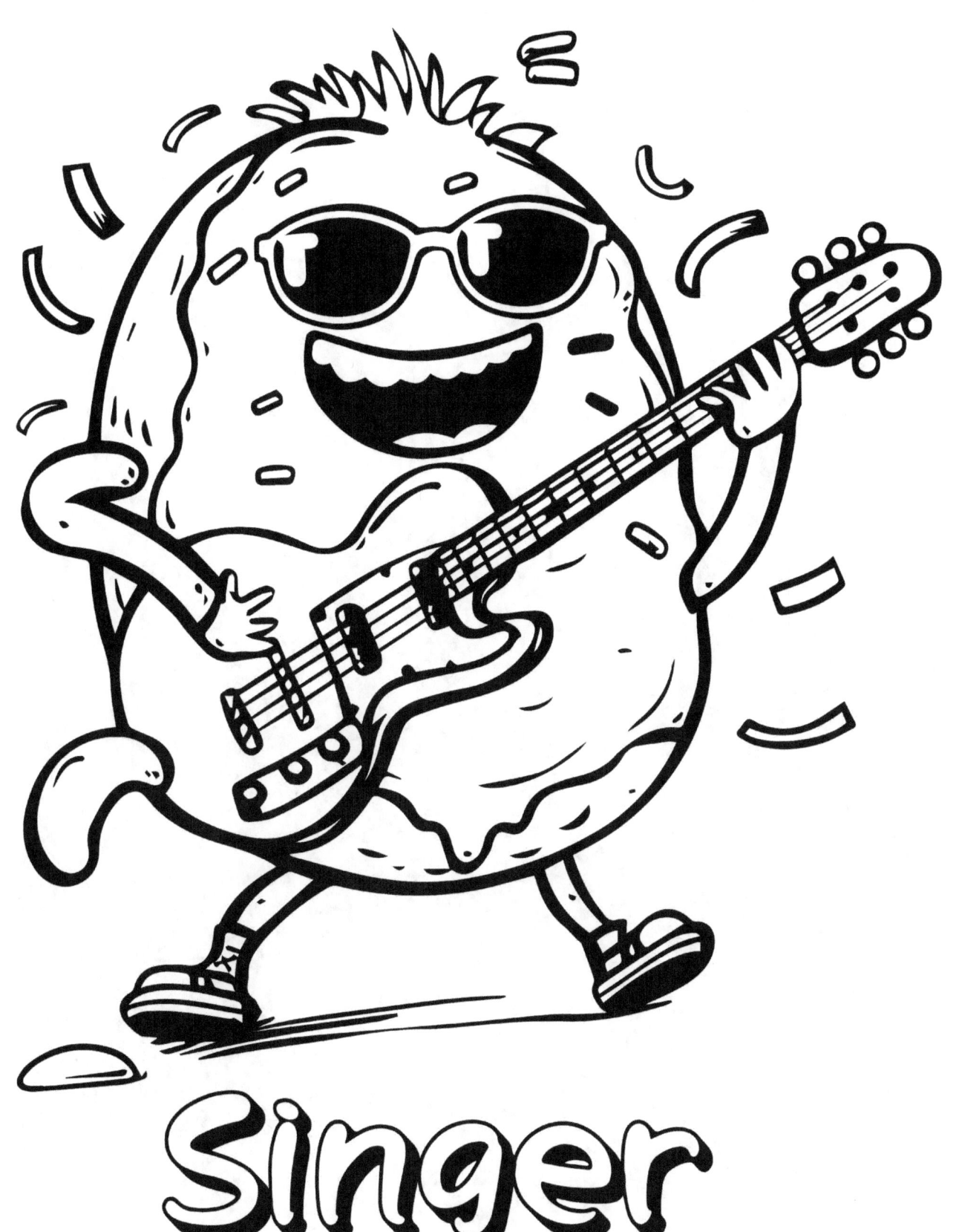

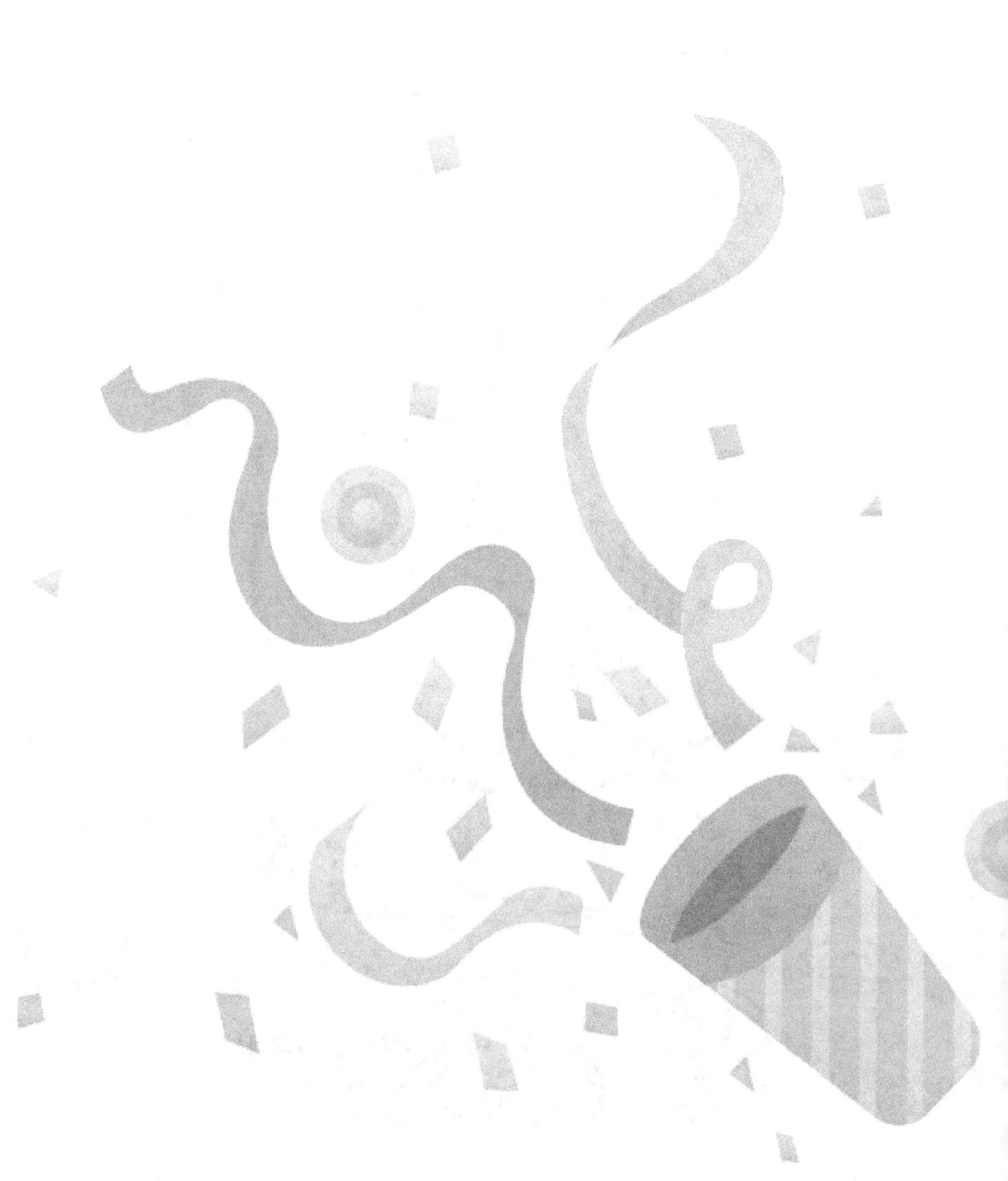

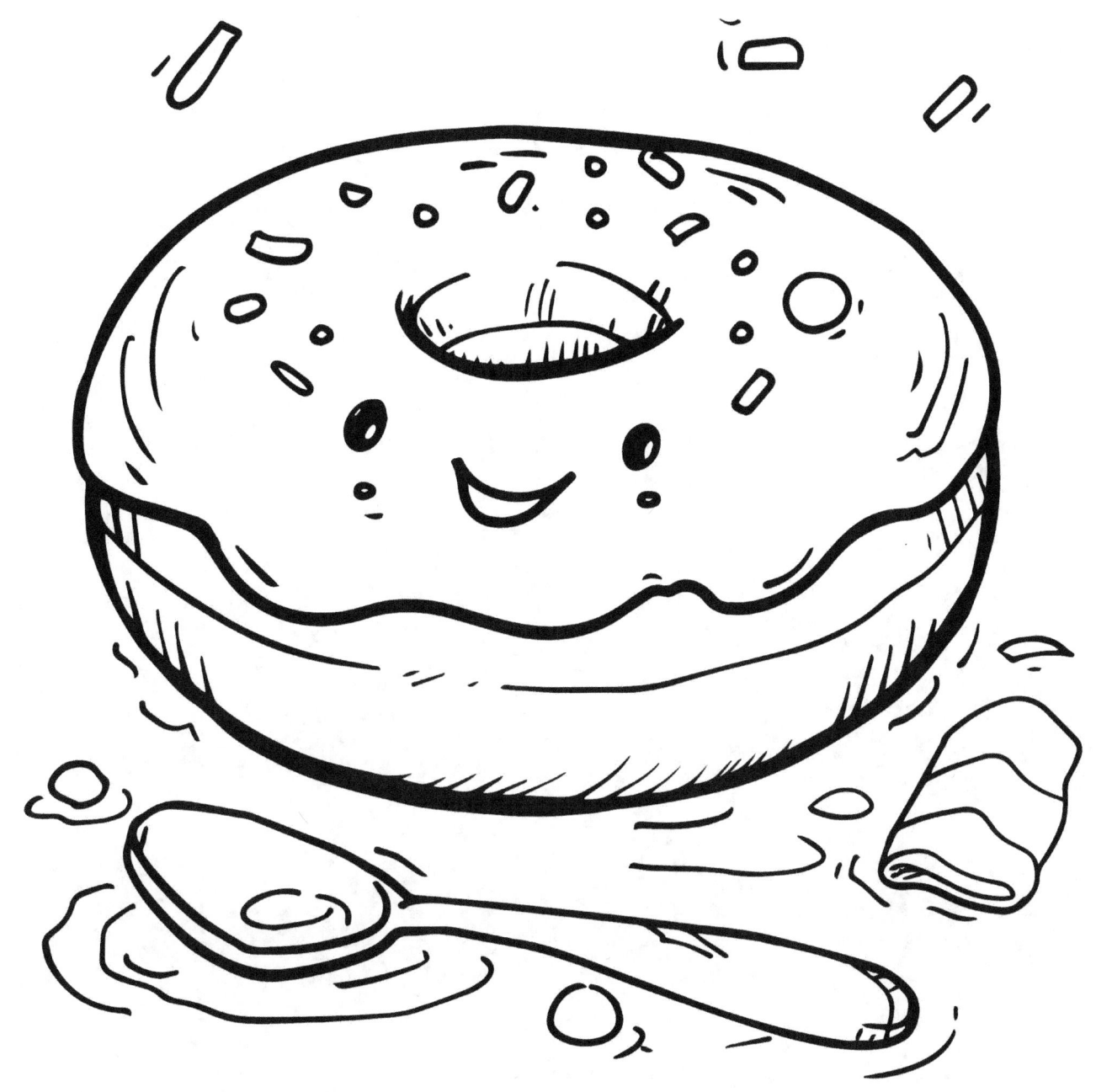

Bathe

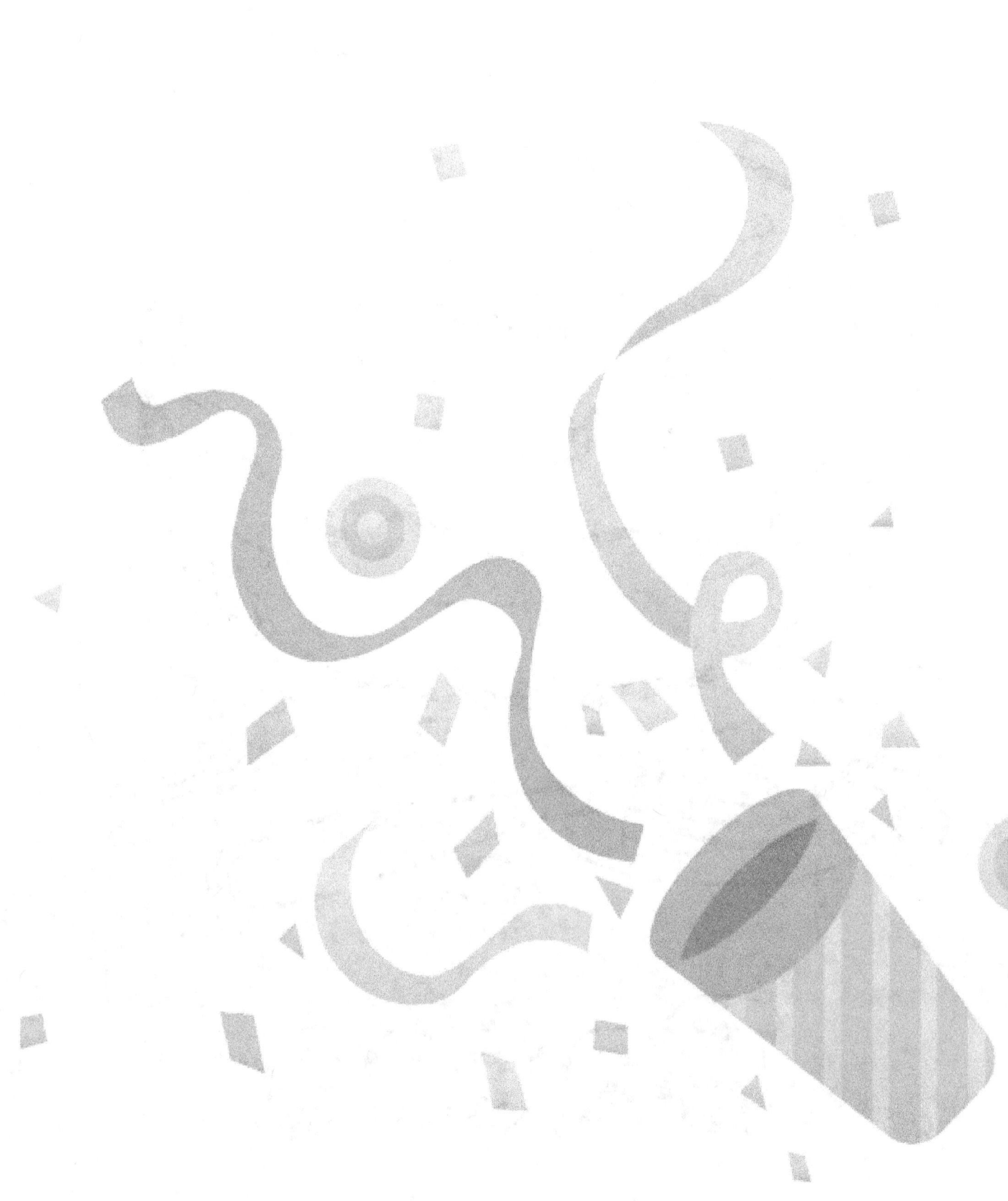

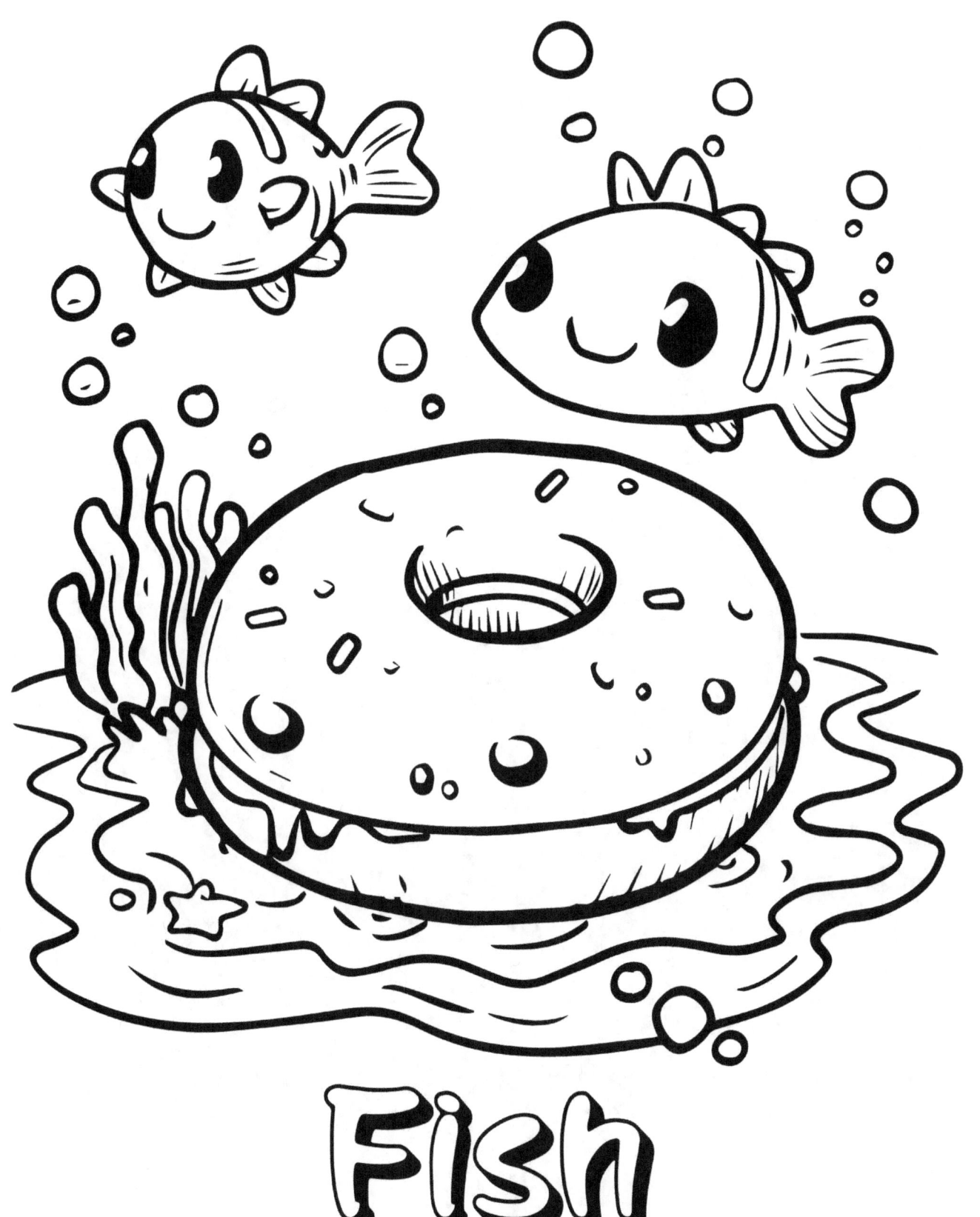

Fish

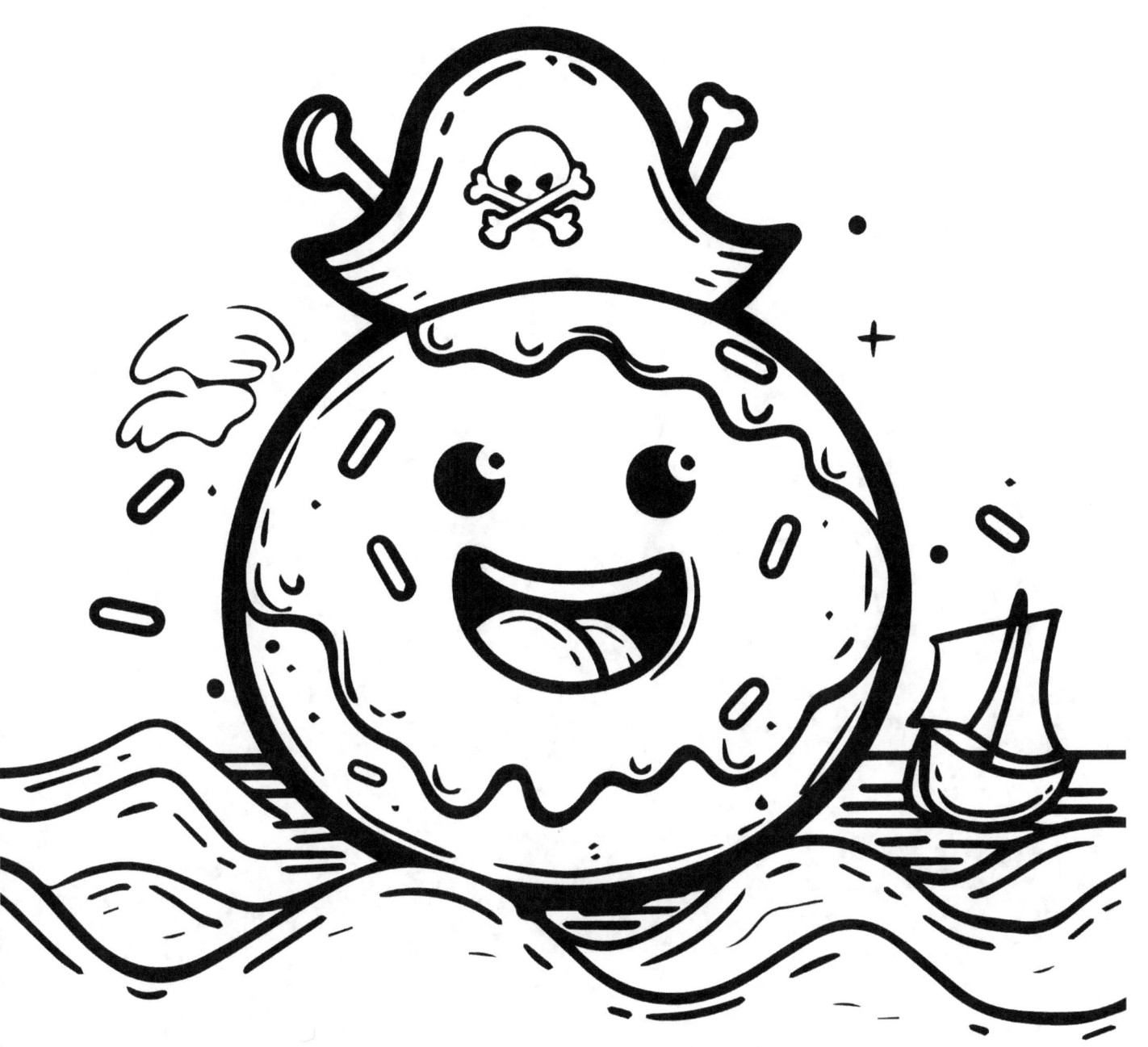

Pirate

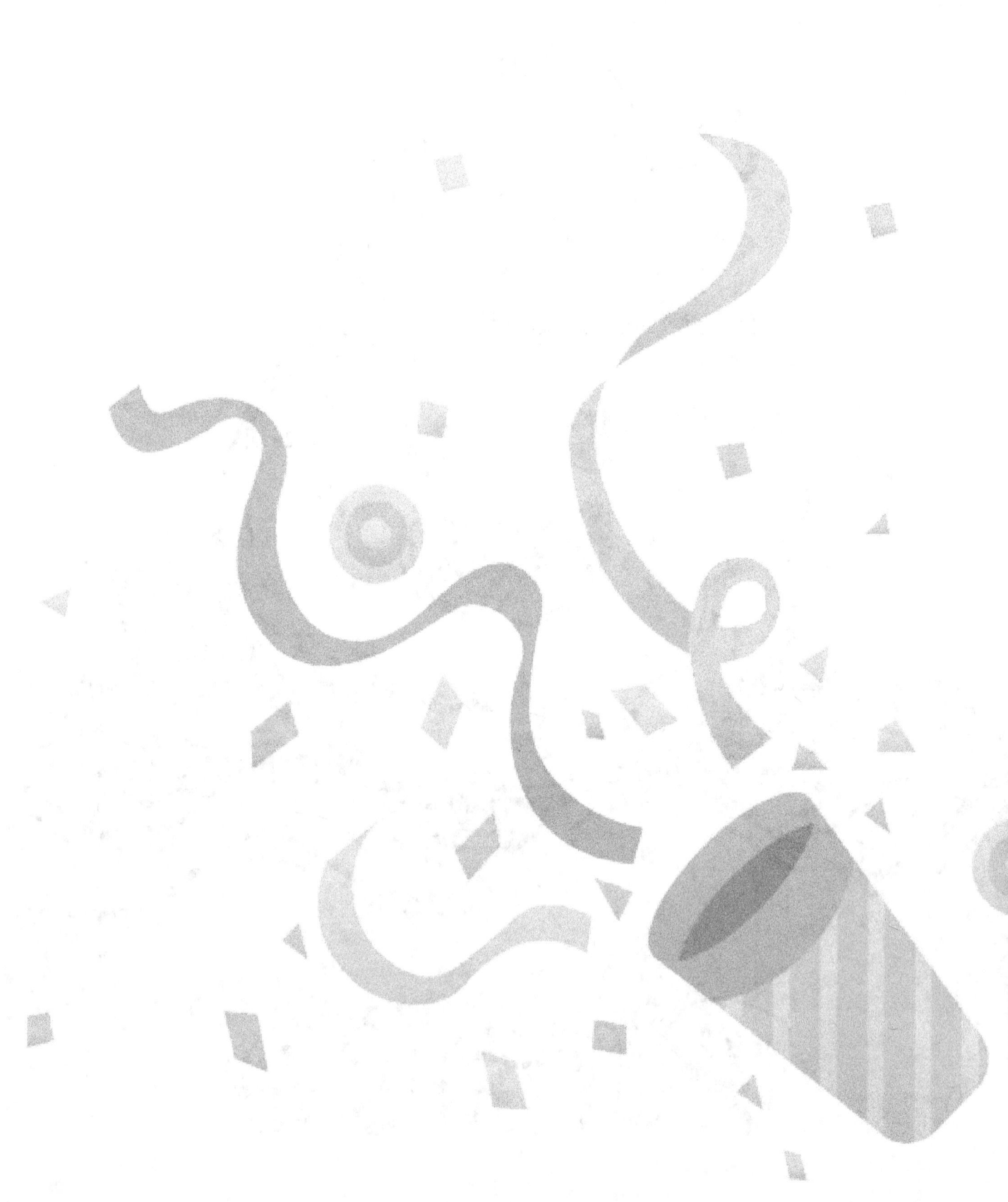

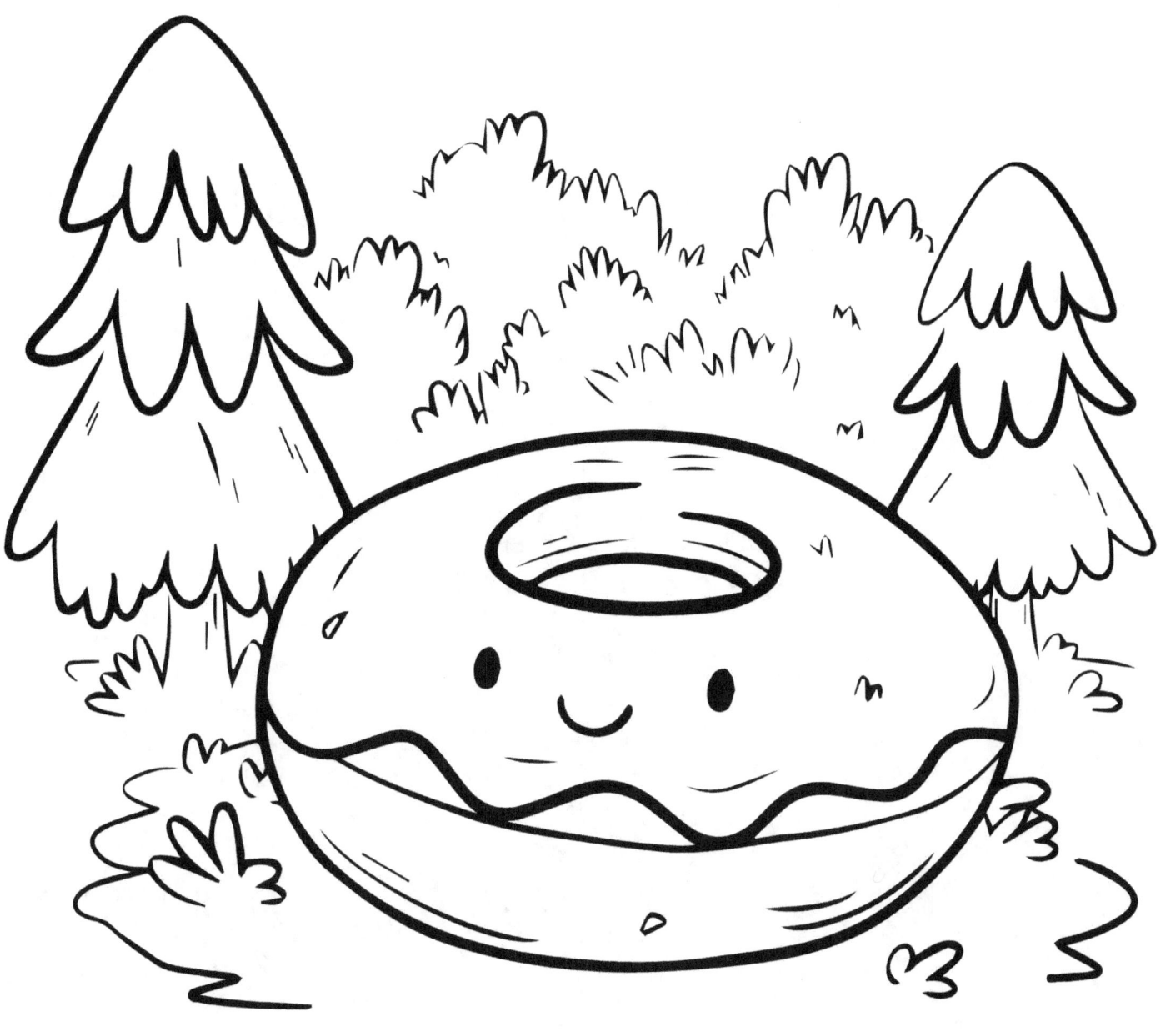

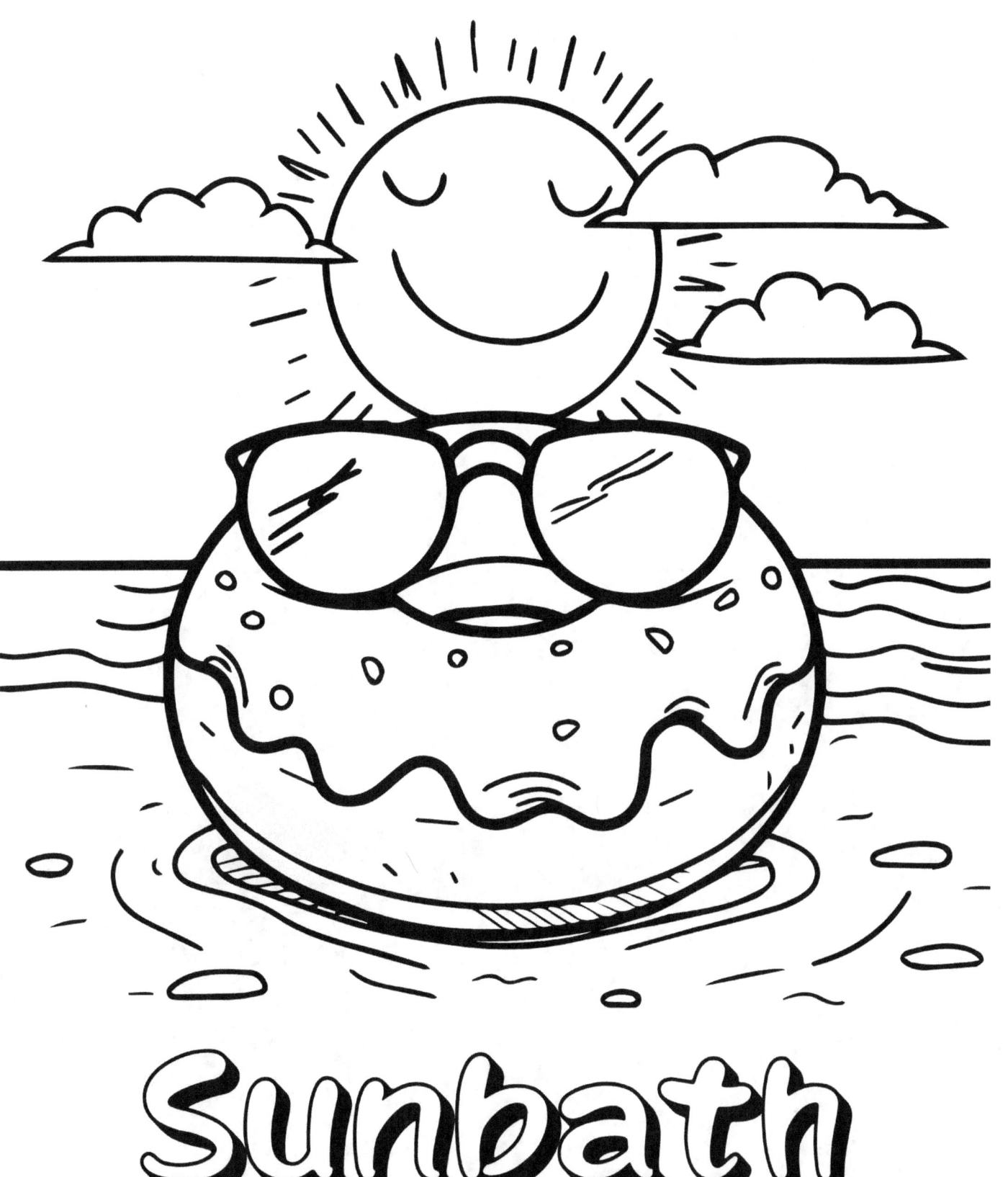

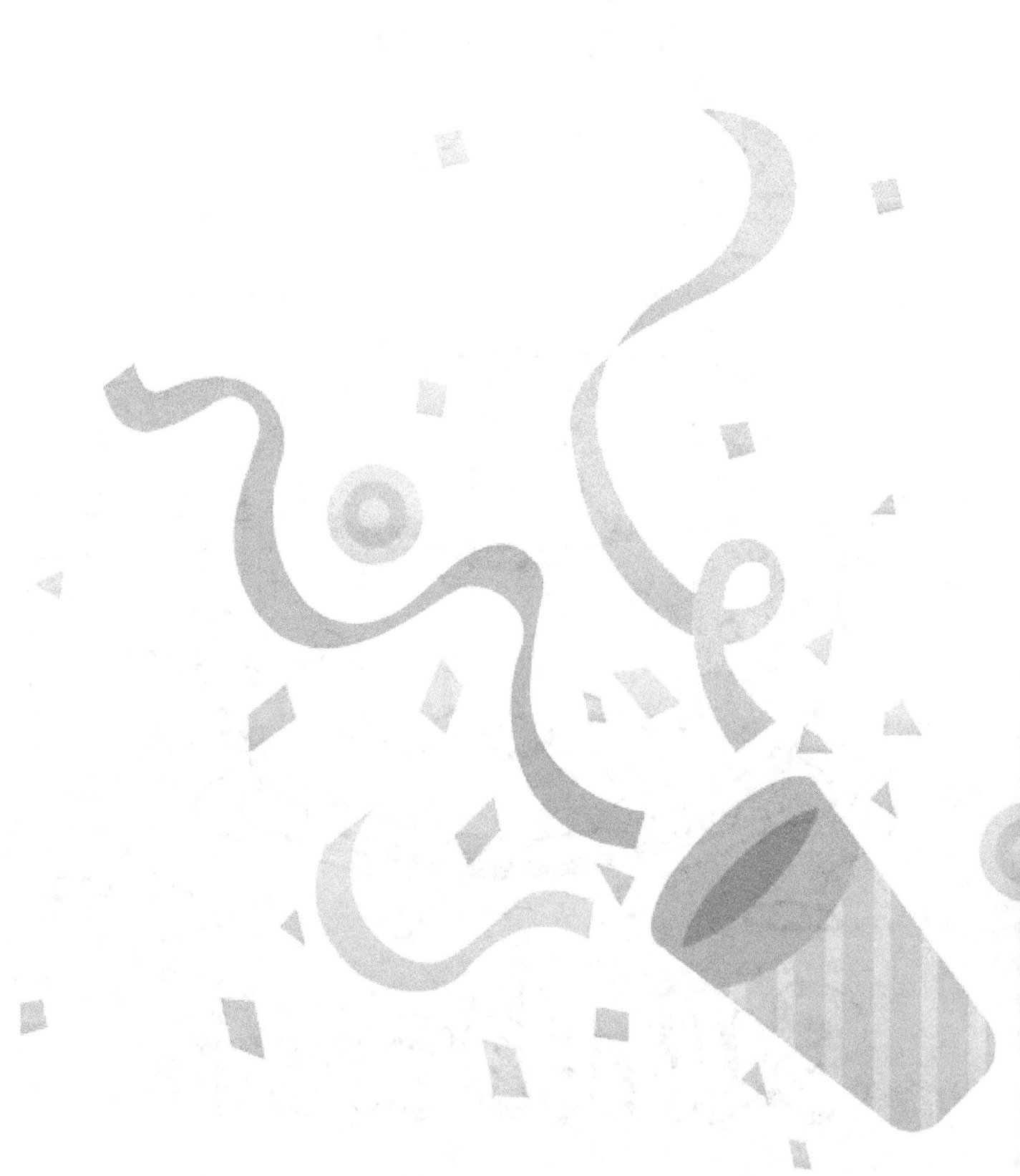

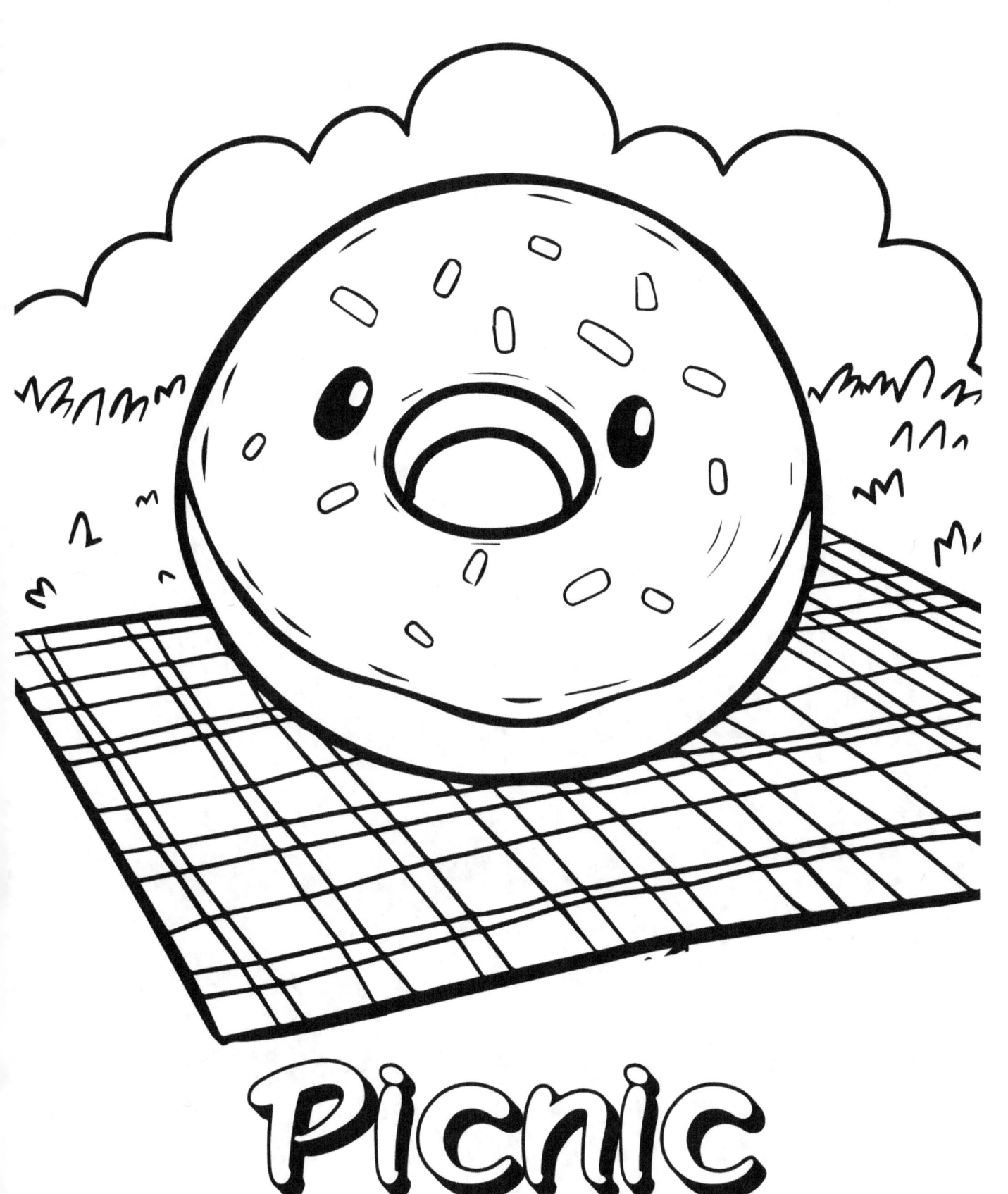

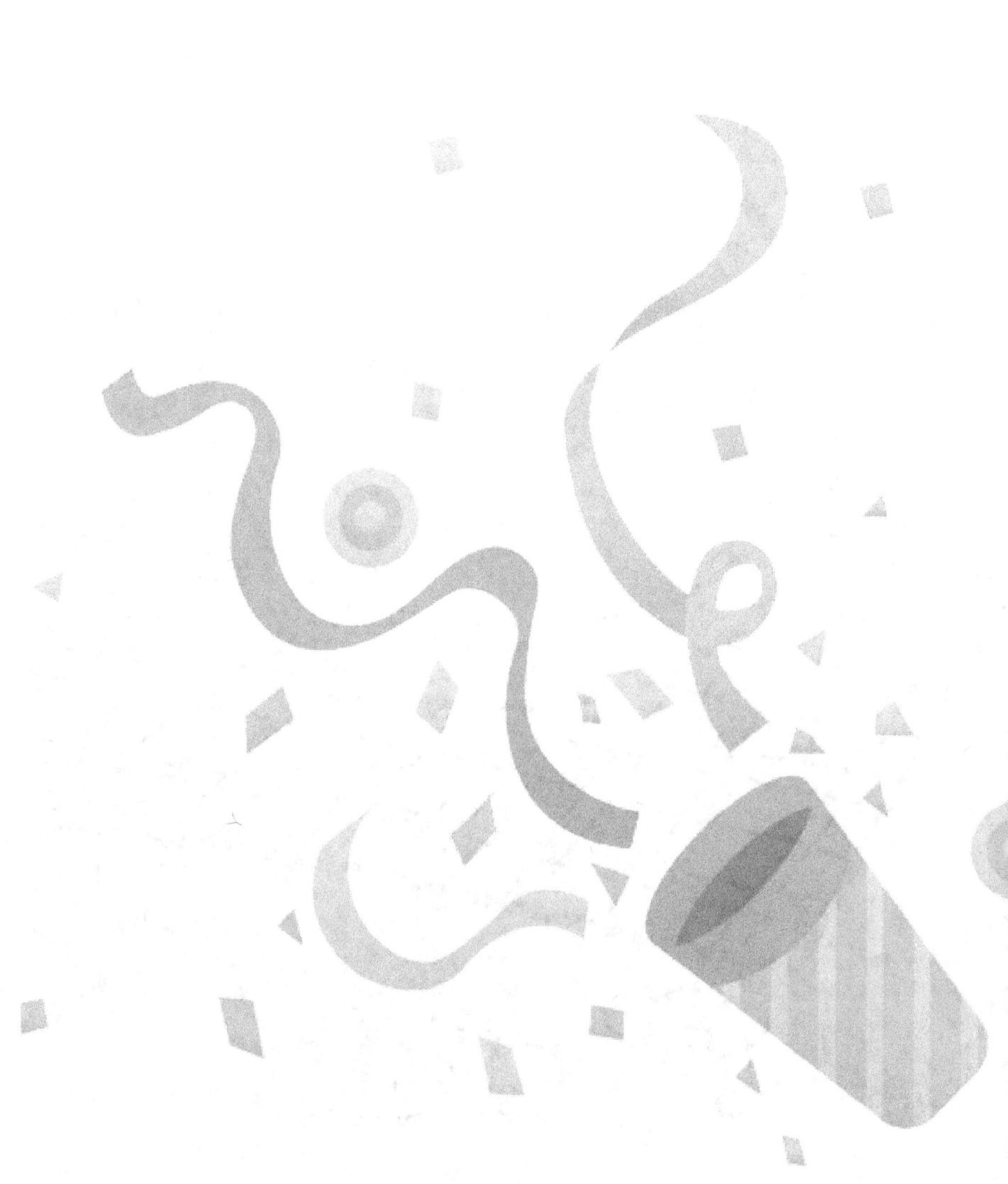

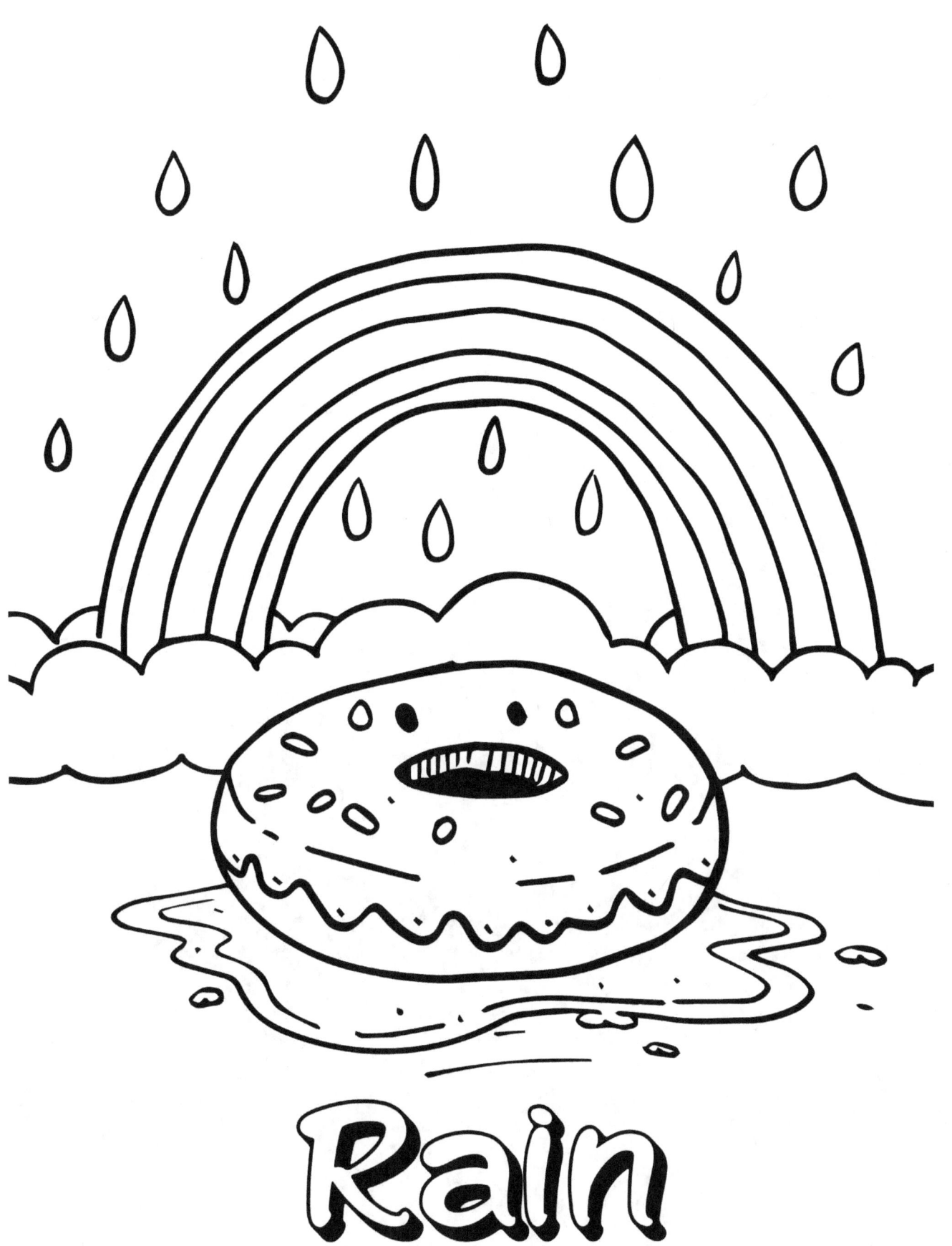

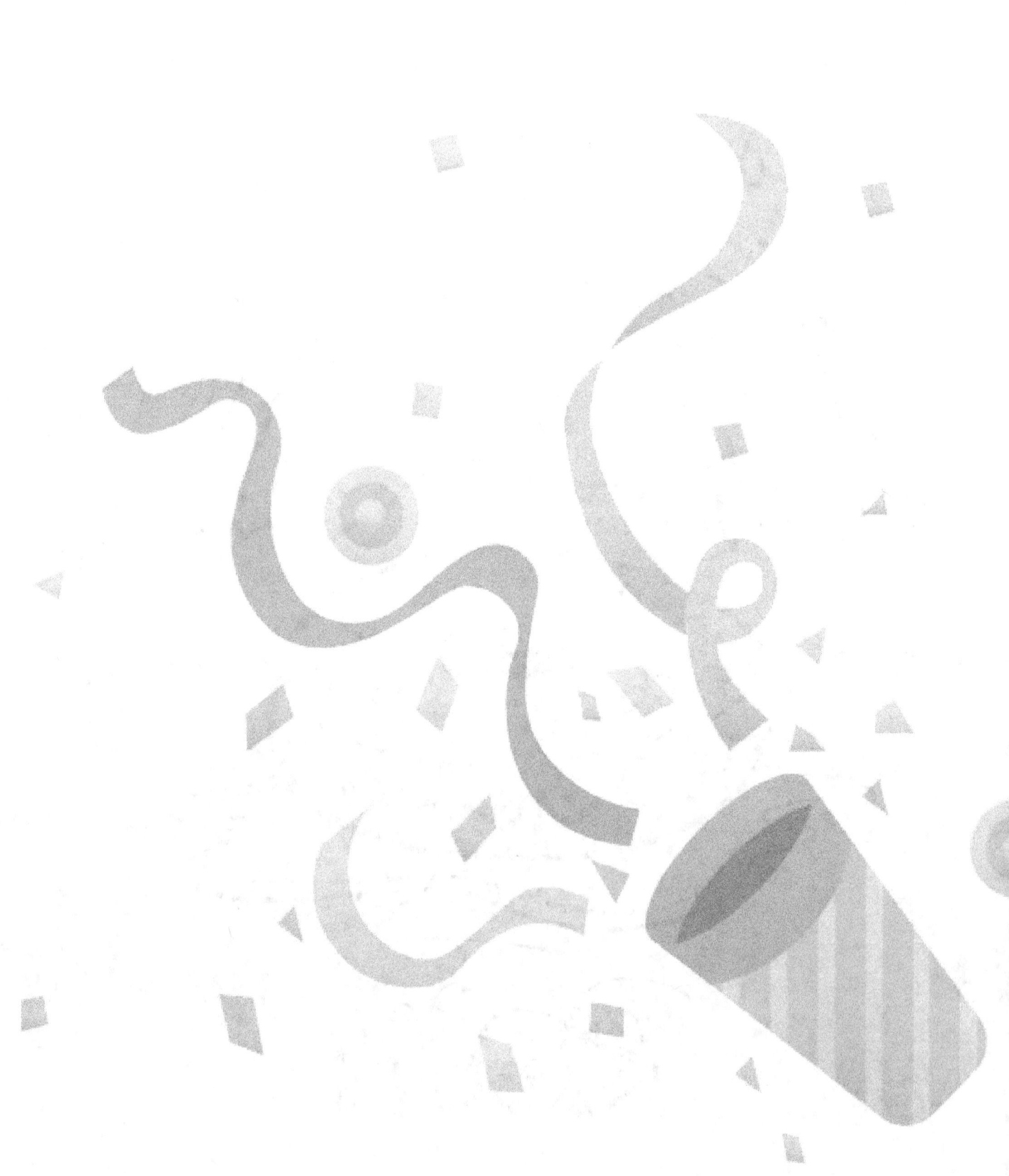

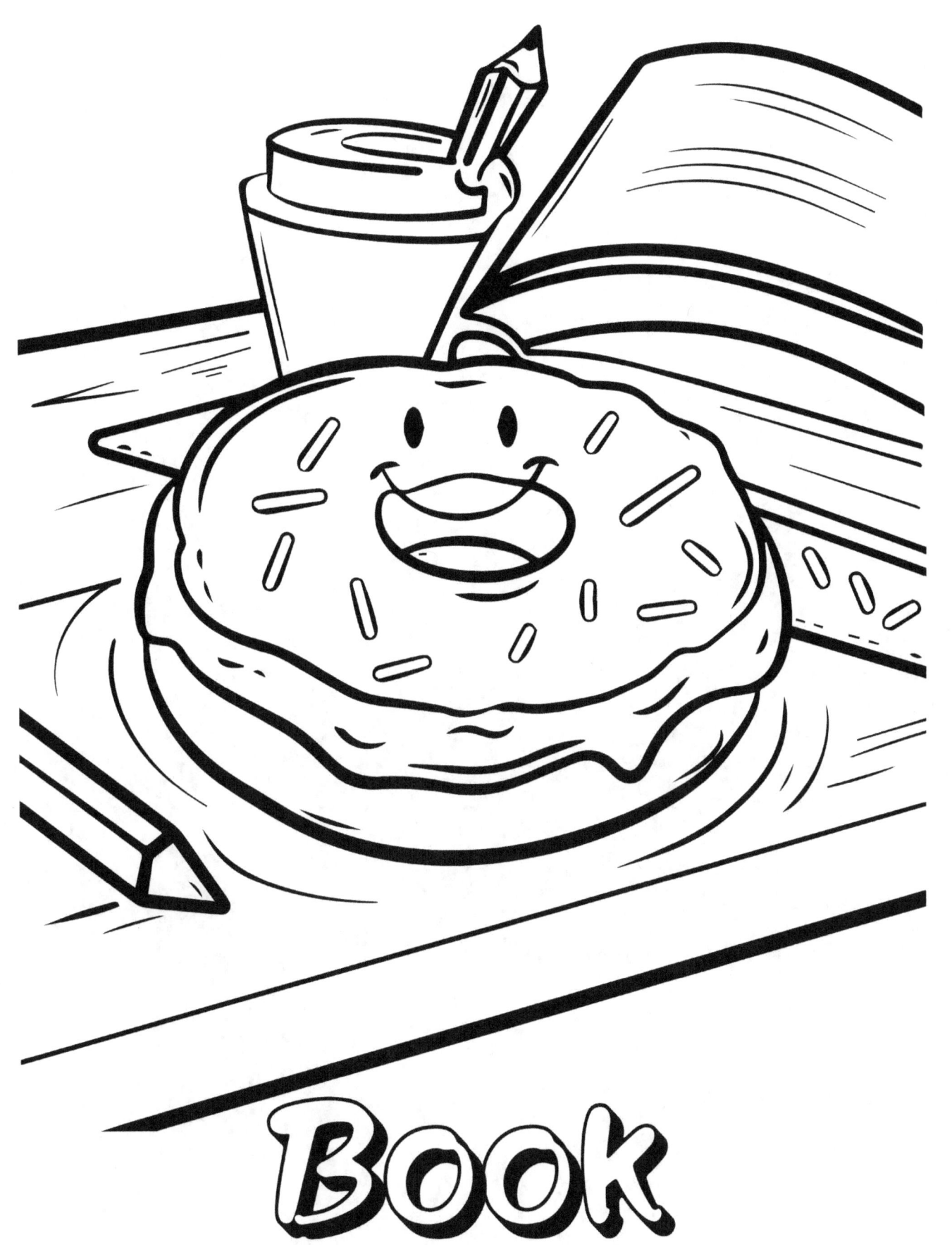

Book

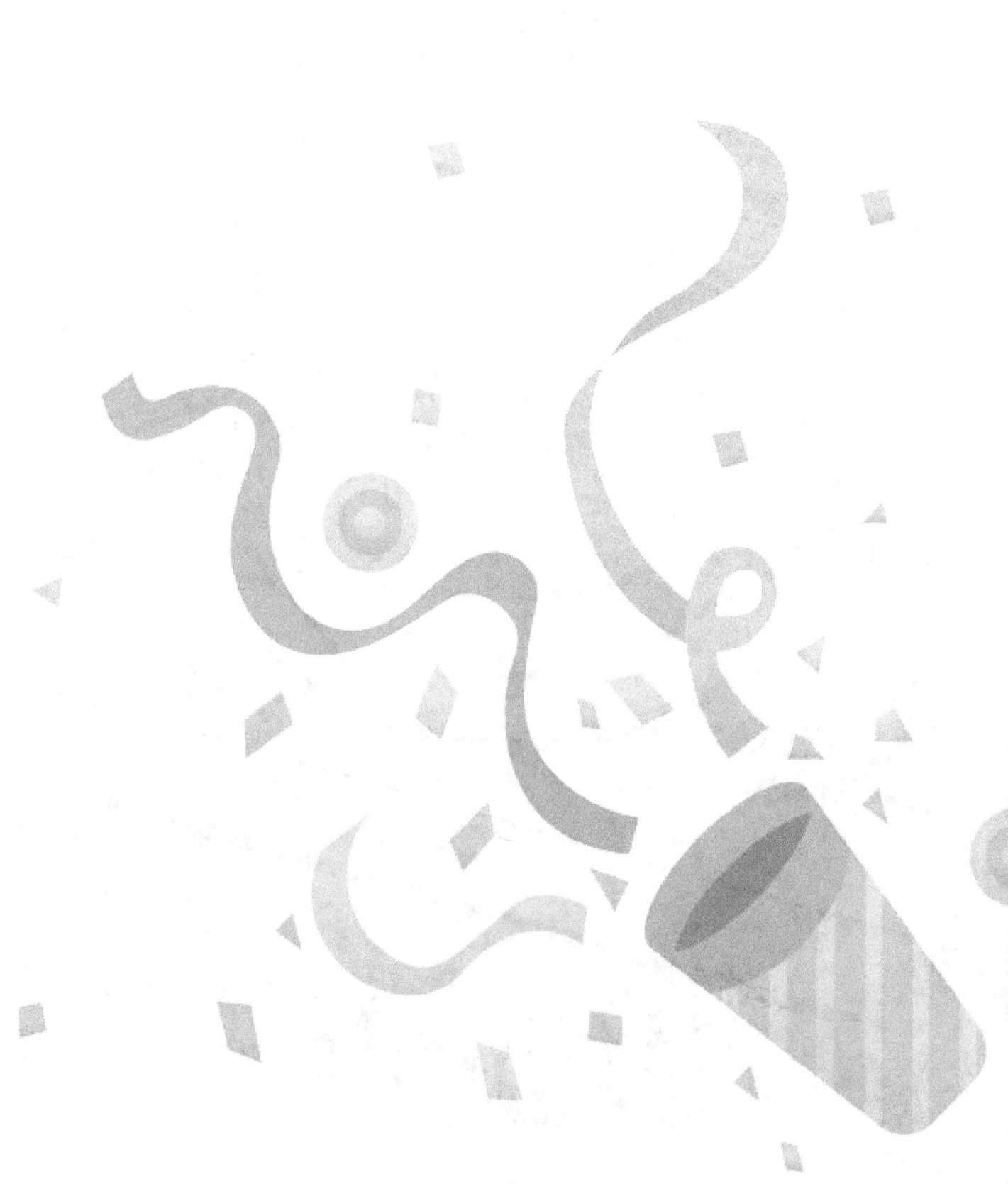

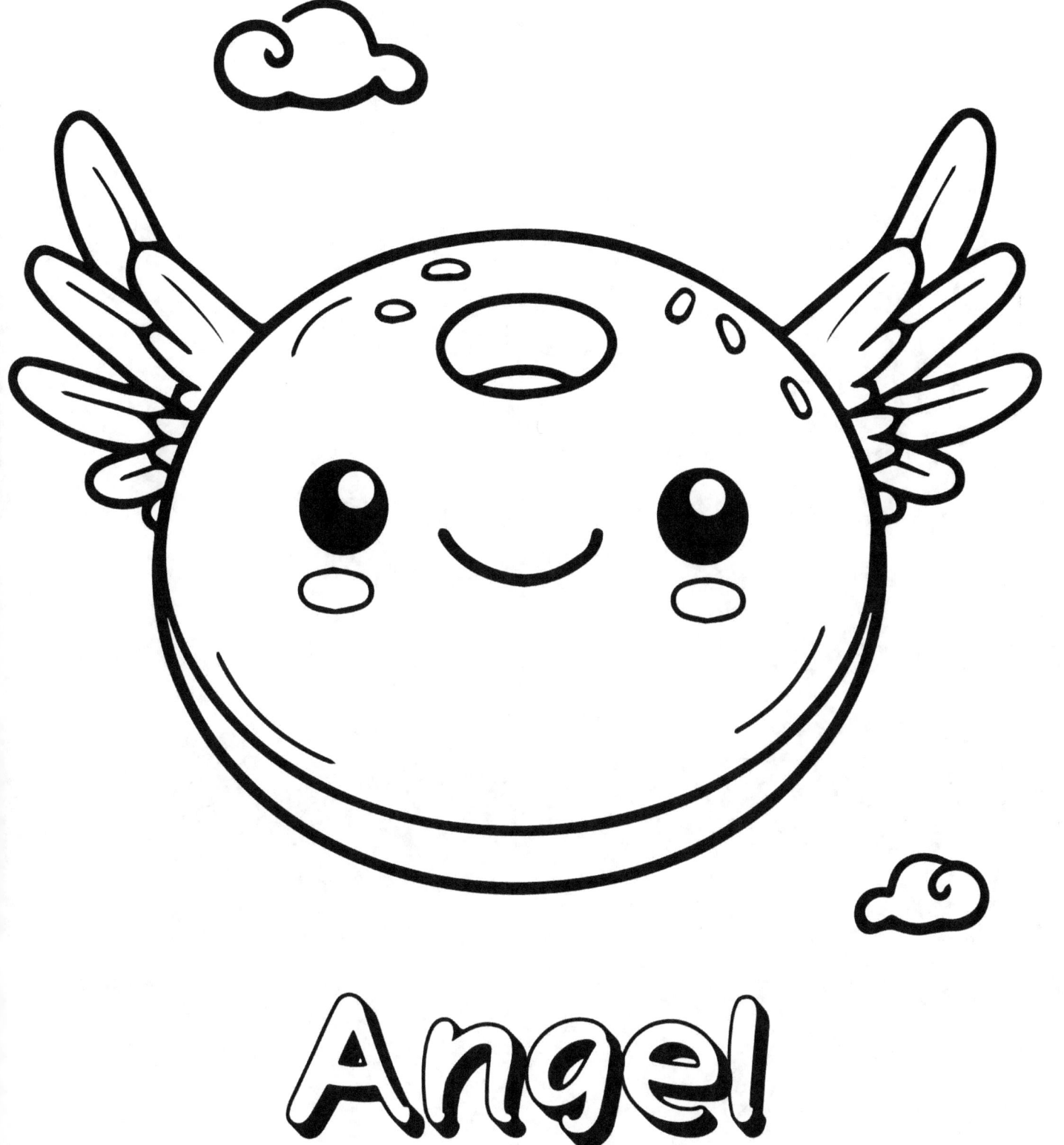

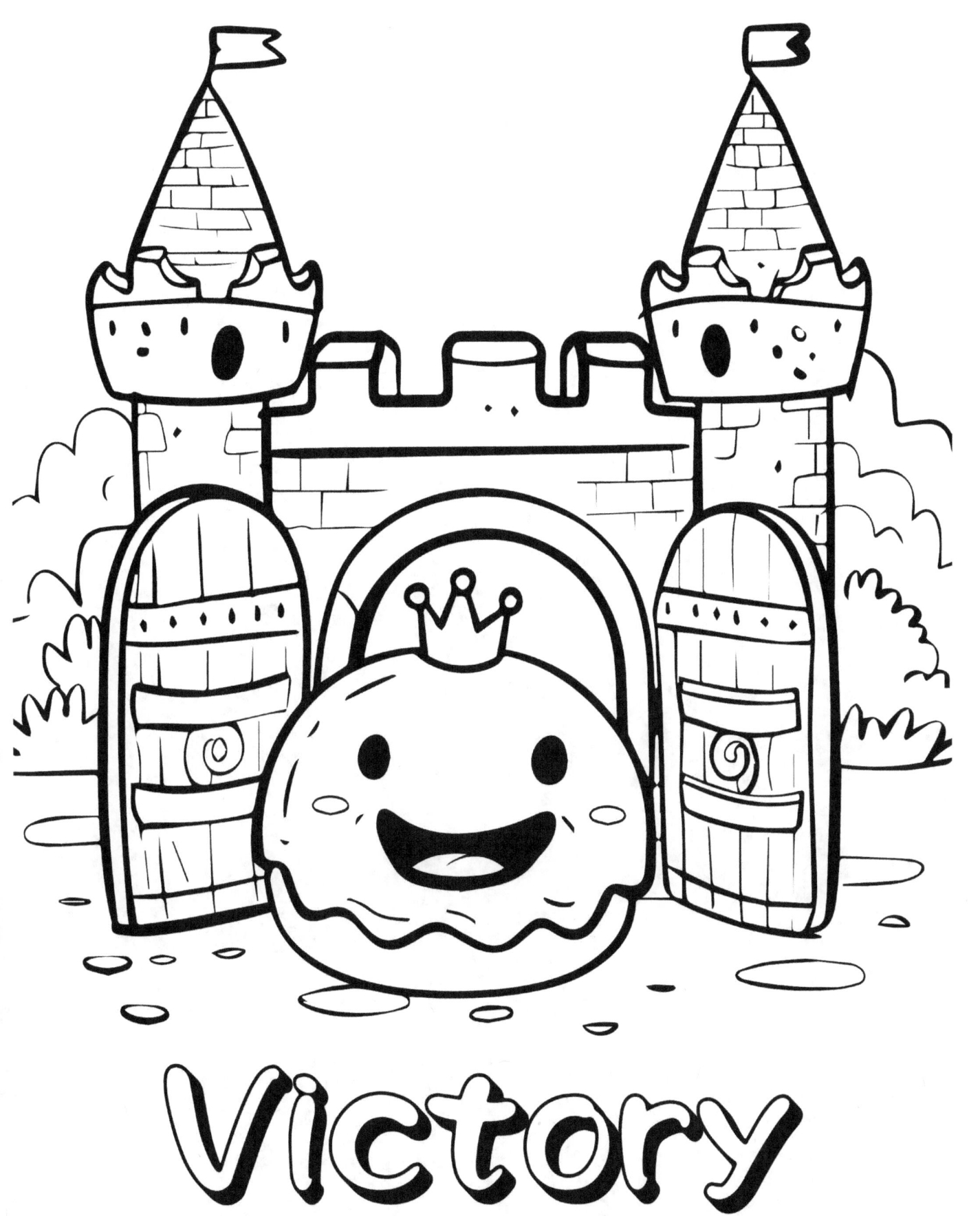

www.ingramcontent.com/pod-product-compliance
Lightning Source LLC
Chambersburg PA
CBHW062124220526
45471CB00010B/3876